Resorts of the Catskills

Resorts of the Catskills

Color Photography by John Margolies

Essays by Alf Evers, Elizabeth Cromley,
Betsy Blackmar, and Neil Harris

The Architectural League of New York
The Gallery Association of New York State

St. Martin's Press, Inc., New York

This publication and accompanying exhibition are made possible with public funds from the National Endowment for the Humanities, a Federal Agency, the New York Council for the Humanities, and the New York State Council on the Arts.

Library of Congress Catalog Card No. 79-65868

Printed in the United States of America.

Book design: William Padgett, Syracuse and Kevan Moss
Archival photos: Courtney Frisse, Syracuse

A JEFFREY WEISS BOOK

To Alf Evers

Contents

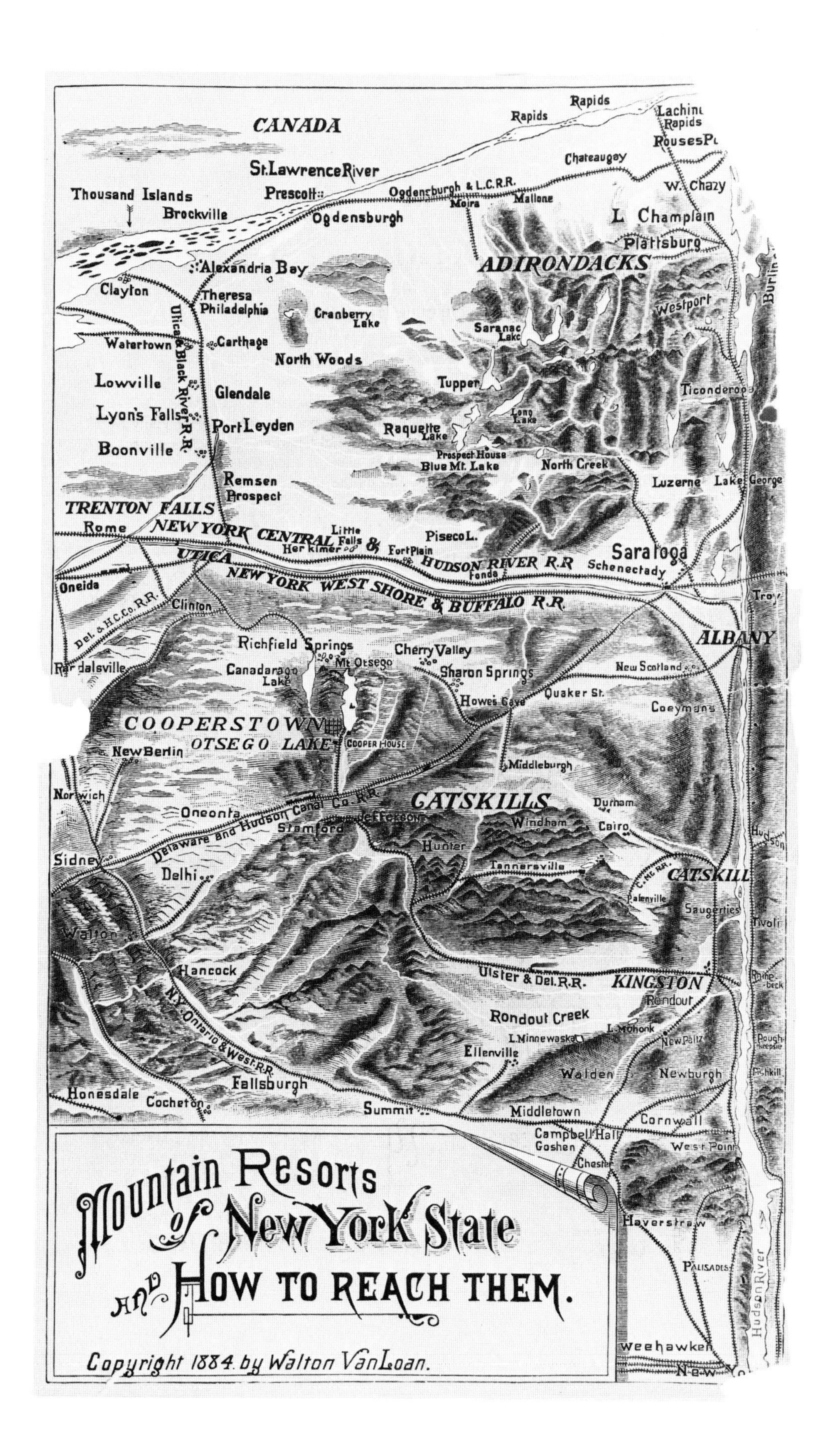

Mountain Resorts of New York State and How to Reach Them.
Copyright 1884. by Walton VanLoan.
CANADA
St. Lawrence River
Thousand Islands
Brockville
Prescott
Ogdensburgh
Ogdensburgh & L.C.R.R.
Moira
Mallone
Chateaugay
Rapids
Rapids
Lachine Rapids
Rouses Pt
W. Chazy
L Champlain
Plattsburg
ADIRONDACKS
Alexandria Bay
Clayton
Theresa
Philadelphia
Cranberry Lake
Saranac Lake
Westport
Watertown
Carthage
Utica & Black River R.R.
North Woods
Lowville
Glendale
Tupper
Ticonderoga
Lyon's Falls
Port Leyden
Raquette Lake
Long Lake
Boonville
Prospect House
Blue Mt. Lake
North Creek
Luzerne
Lake George
Remsen
Prospect
TRENTON FALLS
Rome
NEW YORK CENTRAL & HUDSON RIVER R.R.
Little Falls
Herkimer
Fort Plain
Piseco L.
Saratoga
Schenectady
Fonda
UTICA
Oneida
NEW YORK WEST SHORE & BUFFALO R.R.
Clinton
Del. & H.C. Co. R.R.
Troy
ALBANY
Richfield Springs
Cherry Valley
Sharon Springs
Mt. Otsego
New Scotland
Randalsville
Canadarago Lake
Quaker St.
Howe's Cave
Coeymans
COOPERSTOWN
OTSEGO LAKE
COOPER HOUSE
New Berlin
Middleburgh
Norwich
CATSKILLS
Durham
Oneonta
Delaware and Hudson Canal Co. R.R.
Jefferson
Stamford
Windham
Cairo
Hunter
Sidney
Tannersville
Delhi
CATSKILL
Palenville
Saugerties
Walton
Tivoli
Hancock
Ulster & Del. R.R.
KINGSTON
Rondout
Rondout Creek
N.Y. Ontario & West. R.R.
L. Minnewaska
L. Mohonk
New Paltz
Ellenville
Walden
Newburgh
Fallsburgh
Honesdale
Cochecton
Summit
Middletown
Cornwall
Campbell Hall
Goshen
Chester
West Point
Haverstraw
PALISADES
Hudson River
Weehawken
New York

Acknowledgments

This project began with the work of John Margolies, whose photographs and video work on the Catskill resorts provided the focus for an unusual combination of popular and scholarly interests. The collaboration of historians Elizabeth Cromley, Betsy Blackmar, Alf Evers, and Neil Harris with John was exemplary, because as a group they displayed an expansiveness and a sense of adventure in supplying the critical and interpretive context for this subject.

The association of The Architectural League of New York and the Gallery Association of New York State was also fortuitous: The League's aim to encourage innovative projects in architecture and related art areas was supported by the Association's skilled assistance in the development and design of this exhibition for public institutions in New York. We are especially grateful to our Boards of Directors, colleagues whose collective vision and purpose has facilitated the sponsorship of a particularly challenging venture.

We are especially thankful to those who worked to find ways to realize the subject's visual and interpretive presentation for a large public audience: Kevan Moss, the Association's Director of Exhibitions and designer of the exhibition, Sara Blackburn, editor, and Jeffrey Weiss, publishing consultant.

Financial assistance and encouragement from the staff and advisers of federal and state funding agencies has been essential at every point. John Margolies's work was initially supported by the New York State Council on the Arts's Architectural and Environmental Arts division under the direction of Coco Eiseman, and the early stages of shaping this project were buttressed by funds from the New York Council for the Humanities under the direction of Dr. Carol Groneman.

In creating *Resorts of the Catskills*, it has been the generosity of the National Endowment for the Humanities, the New York State Council on the Arts, and the New York Council for the Humanities that has made this project possible.

Another overriding acknowledgment must, of course, be to the hotel owners, residents of the area, and historian Alf Evers. The Catskills is their place. To the extent that this project presumes to record and interpret its history, we all resort to them—their guests and fellow vacationers.

—*Trudy C. Kramer*
Executive Director
Gallery Association of New York State

—*Jonathan Barnett*
President
Architectural League of New York

Much of the history of the Catskill resorts lies embedded in the memories of the resort owners and guests. We would like to thank the countless people who shared information and personal anecdotes with us. We hope they will recognize themselves in the story we have told. We also owe a special debt to those people who helped us translate the social traditions of Catskill resorts into the exhibit and these essays.

We are grateful to the following for recounting their Catskill experiences: Milton Brown; Bernard and Gladys Leon; Melvin Mayes; John and Lynn Weiner; Dennis Jurow; and all the hotel and resort owners.

The resources of the following institutions were especially useful in doing the research on the architectural and social history of the region: Albany Institute of History and Art, Albany, N.Y.; Avery Library, Columbia University, New York, N.Y.; State Library at Albany, Albany, N.Y.; Bronck House, Greene County Historical Society, Coxsackie, N.Y.; Catskill Center for Conservation and Development, Hobart, N.Y.; Cooper-Hewitt Museum of Design, New York, N.Y.; Durham Center Museum, Durham, N.Y. ; Ellenville Public Library, Ellenville, N.Y.; Haines Falls Free Library, Haines Falls, N.Y.; Hope Farm Bookshop, Cornwallville, N.Y.; Kingston Senate House Library, Kingston, N.Y.; Mohonk Barn Museum, New Paltz, N.Y.; Print and Manuscript Collections, New York Historical Society, New York, N.Y.; Local History, Print and Manuscript Collections, New York Public Library, New York, N.Y.; Hotel School and Library, State University of New York, College at Delhi; Department of Art History, State University of New York, College at New Paltz; Tamiment Labor Library, New York University, New York, N.Y.

The private collections most valuable to us were the Manville Wakefield Collection and Barbara Purcell, Grahamsville, N.Y.; the Alf Evers Collection, Shady, N.Y.; and those of Betty Y. O'Hara, Prattsville, N.Y.; Richard Vindigni, Villa Roma, Callicoon, N.Y.; Bernard and Gladys Leon, New York, N.Y.; and Sadie Kotler, New York, N.Y.

We are deeply appreciative of the unfailing interest and encouragement throughout the project of Alf Evers, Neil Harris, and Sara Blackburn. For professional advice, we are also grateful to Jonathan Barnett and Marita O'Hare of the Architectural League of New York; Peter Borrelli and Thomas Miner of the Catskill Center for Conservation and Development, Hobart, N.Y.; Ben Kaplan of the Public Information Office of Sullivan County; Barbara Coker and Steve Finkle of the Greene County Office of Development; Rose Cairns of the Delaware County Chamber of Commerce; and Leon Stein, editor emeritus of *Justice* of the ILGWU.

We appreciate critical readings of the catalog essays in the early stages by Warren Leon, Roy Rosenzweig, Michael Jaker, and Jack Greenhut, and the work of Lona Foote, who helped with the research, interviews, and photographic selections and added a valuable perspective to shaping the project. Special thanks must go to Skip Blumberg, co-producer of the video tape *Resorts of the Catskills*; to Andy Aaron, Bill Marpet, and Esti Marpet for their helpful assistance; and to the New York State Council on the Arts, the John R. Jakobson Foundation, and the Architectural League of New York for their financial support.

We extend our thanks for consultation to Joseph O'Grady, Thomas Kershner, Edwin Schlossberg, Robert Twombly, Deborah Nevins, Joan Brumberg, Keith Crandell, William Rhoads, Dale Stein, Justine Hommel, Arthur Rashap, Judith Paine, Barbara Matalavage, Charles Dornbush, Helen Crowley, Vernon Haskins, Raymond Beecher, and E. Buttons Ryan; and to Deborah Gardner and Brian Danforth for their helpful assistance.

We wish to acknowledge the following for their talent and guidance in producing the exhibition and publication: Trudy Kramer, Kevan Moss, John Matherly, Carol Kinne, Patricia Ford, and Stephen Horne of the Gallery Association; John MacDonald; Keith Metzler of the New York State Museum; Courtney Frisse; Bruce Parker; Ray Santola; Eugene Canfield; William Padgett; the Canterbury Press and St. Martin's Press.

Our special thanks to the resorts of today's Catskills, whose hospitality, generous offerings of information and time, scrapbooks, and memories made this project possible: Antonio's Twin Mountain House, Elka Park; Bavarian Manor, Cairo; The Hotel Brickman, South Fallsburg; Brown's Hotel, Loch Sheldrake; The Concord, Kiamesha Lake; Edgewood Inn, Livingston Manor; The Fallsview, Ellenville; Gavin's Golden Hill House, East Durham; The Granit, Kerhonkson; Grossinger's Grossinger; Hanson's Hotel, Deposit; Homowack Lodge, Spring Glen; Huff House, Roscoe; Kutsher's Country Club, Kiamesha Lake; Lake Minnewaska Mountain Houses, New Paltz; Meinstein's Lodge, Fleischmanns; Menges' Lakeside, Livingston Manor; Mohonk Mountain House, Lake Mohonk, New Paltz; Mountain Lake Manor, Bloomington; Nevele Hotel and Country Club, Ellenville; The Pines, South Fallsburg; The Raleigh, South Fallsburg; Rosa del Monte, Haines Falls; Scott's Oquaga Lake House, Deposit; Stevensville Country Club, Swan Lake; Sugar Maples, Maplecrest; Tennanah Lake Shore Lodge, Roscoe; Thompson House, Windham; White Roe Lake House, Livingston Manor; Villa Maria, Haines Falls; Villa Roma, Callicoon; Windham House, Windham; Winter Clove, Round Top.

—Betsy Blackmar
—Elizabeth Cromley
—John Margolies

August, 1979

Introduction

Throughout history we have tended to assign greater value to the unique and the monumental, ignoring the importance of everyday experience —what we share in common. Traditional definitions are no longer applicable to the quality of contemporary experience. Instead of dealing with architecture as the work of great masters, my work for the past 10 years has been concerned with the documenting and analyzing of everyday, vernacular architecture—how people live, where they go, and what they do as they interact with their environment.

This study of the Catskill resorts is an outgrowth of my interest in one aspect of vernacular design: the architectural expression of hotels, motels, and resorts. In the 1970 exhibition, "Morris Lapidus: Architecture of Joy," I explored the popular phenomenon of the Miami Beach hotel. In the fall of 1973, I documented, by an article with photographs, the Madonna Inn in San Luis Obispo, California *(Progressive Architecture*, November, 1973). The inn is an extraordinary architectural monument designed by a non-architect; each of its 109 guest rooms expresses a separate, thematic fantasy environment. These concerns were expanded upon in a series of photographs *(Esquire*, July 1976) demonstrating the iconic sameness of franchised motel chains.

When I first began working in the Catskill region of New York State in the summer of 1976, I expected to find contemporary facilities similar to those in Miami Beach and the franchised motels. What surprised me then, and has continued to surprise me as I photographed the region in 1977 and 1978, was the range of resort types from the past 150 years which has survived even to the present.

The analysis and interpretation of this hodgepodge of hotels, inns, bungalows, and country clubs was a perplexing problem, since the traditional chronological ordering of history did not fit the Catskill circumstances. At this point, with the invaluable assistance of Trudy Kramer, Executive Director of the Gallery Association of New York State, additional funding was obtained to assemble the team of architectural, social, and regional historians who have helped bring this effort to fruition. Architectural historian Elizabeth Cromley was particularly insightful and helpful throughout the development of this project.

This multi-disciplinary collaboration was very successful and stimulating, and has resulted in what I hope to be a significant contribution to the study of vernacular architecture in general and resort hotels in particular.

—John Margolies
August, 1979

Early Days

The first humans to visit the Catskills were small bands of Indians, drawn to the mountains' oak and beech forests in the fall and early winter to hunt deer, wild turkey, and other game. The animals were fattening there for the cold days ahead on the rich crop of fallen acorns and beechnuts, to be had for the taking. For more than a thousand years, the lower slopes of the outer Catskills served the Indians of the Hudson and Esopus valleys as hunting grounds.

The members of these ancient hunting parties usually camped out in rock shelters, formed when soft layers of bedrock eroded to leave harder layers projecting above. Buried evidence of their Catskill stays still survives beneath the floors of these rock houses — bones of food animals, broken bits of pottery, and tools made of flint and pebbles. The rock shelters were the first human dwellings to appear among the Catskills. Between their era and the nineteenth-century beginnings of the resort hotels which are the subject of *Resorts of the Catskills*, a great deal happened to convert the mountains from a fall and winter hunting ground to a year-round pleasure ground.

The transfer of the Catskills from Indian to white ownership was accompanied by the shattering of the old Indian culture. In accordance with European custom, the English settlers believed they were buying the land on which they settled from the Indians. With no tradition of private ownership of lands, the Indians believed they were merely granting permission for a friendly people to find shelter among them. The "misunderstanding" would lead to deception, murder, and war. Drawn by iron tools, colored cloth, and alcohol to forget their animist traditions and relentlessly pursue beaver, the Indians also accepted bounties to kill the wolves which sometimes raided white settlers' farmyards. They bartered meat and the skins of the deer and bear which thrived along the food-rich line between forest and farmland. In the process of pursuing the beaver, the Indians deepened their mountain trails, and many of these became the basis for the first packhorse routes which eventually expanded into public roads. The beaver ponds, abandoned once their makers were trapped, drew white settlers to farm their fertile, forest-free soil.

When the Indians, weakened by European diseases, alcohol, and other alien enemies against which they had little cultural or biological protection, found themselves pushed back from the rich valleys of their summer settlements, some tried to exist year-round in their seasonal Catskill rock shelters — the hunting or "yagh" houses, as they were known to their Dutch conquerors. Others set up bark-covered huts beside lakes or streams, and there tried, too late, to reestablish their traditional way of life. The "very loving people," whom Robert Juet, Henry Hudson's mate on the *Half Moon*, described in 1609, had no way of suspecting that they would soon become a bewildered and uprooted people.

By the end of the eighteenth century, the Hudson had become recognized as a major American transportation route which made a vast inland region accessible from the city and port of New York. The river had developed its own breed of sailing vessel, superbly adapted to the Hudson's character of a broad estuary with tides felt for a hundred and fifty miles of its length. The capacious, single-masted Hudson River sloops were broad of beam and required crews of only three or four. Skillful boatmen used the tides and winds for the sloops' power, but when these failed, passengers, sometimes equipped with baskets of food and drink, were set ashore to picnic or ramble over the

countryside, gathering wild fruits or nuts until their journeys could resume.

By this time European landscape romanticism had made England's Lake District, the Rhine, and the Alps into leading attractions for those European travelers who had learned to enjoy the sublime and picturesque aspects of the natural world. The same wave of romanticism touched Americans, turning the Hudson into a similarly magic and fashionable region. Sloop captains entertained their passengers with local lore and legends, transforming the trip up the river into a cultural and recreational adventure. The captains pointed out sites on the riverbanks which were acquiring a certain glamour because they had been the scenes of stirring incidents in the Revolutionary War. With the fiftieth anniversary of American independence approaching, such places were beginning to glow with patriotic interest as well as romantic charm. The Catskills took their place in the cluster of romantic sights to be enjoyed by sloop passengers.

In 1813, Horatio Gates Spafford's *A Gazetteer of the State of New-York* was assuring travelers that the Catskills were without an American superior in aesthetic and emotional appeal. "The elegant display of light and shade occasioned by their irregularity," he proclaimed, "their fine blue color, the climbing of the mists up their sides, the intervention of clouds which cap their summits or shroud their sides only, with their occasional reflections from the surface of the Hudson, succeeded by the bursting terrors of their thunder-gusts, all combined... associate a mass of interesting, picturesque and sublime objects, no where exceeded in this country."

Spafford had done his best, but it remained for a much greater writer to capture the essence of the romantic Catskills and to lead the mountains gently and persuasively into the popular consciousness of Americans. Washington Irving's tale "Rip Van Winkle," published in 1819 in *The Sketch Book*, began: "Whoever has made a voyage up the Hudson River must remember the Katskill Mountains," and proceeded to describe "these fairy mountains" and to create for them a human embodiment in Rip Van Winkle, whose marvelous adventures among the Catskills at once became part of the heritage of all English-reading people.

In the same book, Irving wittily expanded on the sport which was becoming closely associated with landscape romanticism—angling. He told of how he had been "bitten by the angling mania" as a youth, with amusing results. The sport came to provide an excuse by which men who felt timid about expressing openly emotional responses to the landscape might nevertheless come into close personal contact with mountains, waterfalls, and moss-covered rocks. Counterparts of Irving's angler, lugging what he described as "a patent rod, a landing net, and a score of other inconveniences, only to be found in the true angler's armory," were continuing to follow streams into the remotest parts of the Catskills. Sullivan County's Beaverkill and Willowemoc creeks were famous among anglers, not only for their abundance of brook trout, but because of their fine scenery.

Before 1800, few people had visited the Catskills purely for enjoyment, but the advent of the steamboat made travel on the Hudson relatively quick and comfortable. And something known in its day as "turnpike fever" began to rage throughout the nation, with a special virulence in the region of the Hudson and the Catskills. New and ambitious roads started pushing out from Hudson River trading towns into the back country of the Catskills and beyond. Their purpose was to steer travelers and

farm and forest products to the riverbank, where all three entities would enhance the profits of local merchants and shippers; absentee landlords and sharp local speculators were hoping that the roads would raise the value of the interior regions they held. But the turnpikes produced another result, comparable to that which similar projects had caused in the England of a few decades earlier. As Christopher Hussey put it in *The Picturesque*, "the appreciation of scenery, the experiencing of romantic emotions, and the perception of the sublime in nature, increased in direct ratio to the number of turnpike acts."

Soon turnpikes had penetrated to many parts of the Catskills: the Susquehanna Turnpike skirted the northern mountains; the Neversink or First Great Southwestern Turnpike ran through Sullivan County; and the Ulster and Delaware Turnpike cut through the center of the region. Among those which were eventually abandoned was the Little Delaware Turnpike, chartered in 1805 to head from the village of Catskill to the mountain wall, scale that wall, and then go on across the Catskills. It passed close to the charmed place where the region's most highly prized natural showpieces were concentrated. These gems were the Kaaterskill Falls, with its two great leaps into a deep and rocky gorge, North and South lakes, with their eerie forest borders, and the Kaaterskill Clove, a stream ornamented with dozens of waterfalls. And to crown it all there was the clifftop known as the Pine Orchard, from which a pilgrim might look out over the Hudson Valley and southern New England into the very heart of infinity.

Inns sprang up along the successful turnpike roads to care for drovers, teamsters, lumbermen, farmers on their way to market, and many others. Those which were favorably located in relation to trout streams became centers for fishermen from far and near. While it lasted, the Little Delaware Turnpike gave fame to one particular inn—that of Colonel Merchant Lawrence, which was placed at the foot of the mountainside that rose steeply to the Pine Orchard. Among the Colonel's regular visitors was James Powers, a young lawyer from the village of Catskill. Late in life, Powers recalled that, early in the nineteenth century, after the labors of the day in his office, he would "drive out to Lawrence's, spend the night there, catch a fine string of trout from the meadow brooks nearby, and then return to town in time for the business of the day." At Lawrence's, Powers delighted in listening to the reminiscences of the old-time hunters who liked to gather there in the evening. They told of stirring encounters with panthers and bear and of notable adventures while hunting deer; they talked of the rattlesnakes which lurked in the mountains, of the deeds of early settlers, of the Indians who had used the Catskills as observation posts and bases for raids during the French and Indian War and the Revolution.

Powers talked, too, with the romantic landscape buffs who used the Lawrence Inn as a base for their expeditions into the mountains, and he realized that such people would welcome more elegant accommodations than Lawrence's could provide. They probably would find it very satisfying to make their base on the Pine Orchard itself, with all the natural wonders of the vicinity within easy reach, he thought.

Powers knew that fine scenery, many waterfalls, and excellent trout fishing prevailed in various regions throughout the country. But nowhere, he realized, were these attractions within such easy reach of large population centers. The accelerated development of transportation on the Hudson, the opening of the turnpikes, the increasing popularity of landscape romanticism, the newly romanticized traditions of Indian and pioneer days, and the safety of the Catskills from the epidemics which from time to time ravaged East Coast and Hudson Valley cities—all these worked together to focus on the Catskill Mountains, and especially on their Pine Orchard, as a place to which Americans might be induced to flock in substantial numbers. Surely, Powers believed, all of this was enough to justify the building of a hotel to care for them. Already a modest resort housed in a "hemlock shanty" had stood on the Pine Orchard and had done well. Joined by like-minded friends in Catskill and by Colonel Lawrence himself, Powers formed a corporation. "The House on the Pine Orchard" which its members built was eventually to become famous as the Catskill Mountain House.

With the opening of the Catskill Mountain House in 1823, the region of the Catskills took its first conspicuous step toward becoming the great resort center which the essays and photographs that follow and the Resorts of the Catskills exhibition celebrate.

—Alf Evers

ALF EVERS, historian and folklorist, is the author of *The Catskills: From Wilderness to Woodstock*, widely acknowledged as the definitive work on the region. He serves as the Town Historian of Woodstock, where he has lived for almost forty years.

A Room with a View

For one hundred fifty years the Catskill Mountains in New York State have served the changing needs of urban Americans seeking a nearby vacation paradise. Their seasonal visits have transformed a hunting and agricultural landscape into an intensely developed tourist mecca. In 1823, the Catskill Mountain House stood alone as a specialized tourist hotel; now bungalow colonies, hotels, country clubs, boarding houses, and motels seem to be virtually everywhere.

The Catskill area is a three-thousand-square-mile, four-county region around the Catskill and Shawangunk mountain ranges. Greene and Delaware counties comprise the northern section of the region, Ulster and Sullivan the southern. The quality of these landscapes is noticeably different from north to south. Nature is rugged in the northern (or "true") Catskills, with abrupt notches between mountains, rushing streams, and numerous waterfalls — small, yet breathtaking. This is the landscape where Romantic Hudson River School painters found an uncultivated eden for their canvases of the 1840s and 1850s. In the south, the Shawangunk range has some equally attractive scenery, but it is less imposing in scale; as one moves west, a lovely undulant landscape replaces mountain peaks with meadows.

Despite the presence of hundreds of resorts, the

HEART OF THE CATSKILLS.

TANNERSVILLE AND THE SURROUNDING MOUNTAINS,

AS SEEN FROM THE SUMMIT OF THE BLACK DOME MOUNTAIN, AT AN ELEVATION OF 4,004 FEET ABOVE TIDE WATER.

1. Black Dome Mountain - - 4,004
2. Hunter Mountain - - - - 4,052
3. Slide Mountain - - - - - 4,220
4. Peakamoose Mountain - - - 3,875
5. Mount Cornell - - - - - 3,920
6. The Wittenberg Mountain - - 3,824
7. East Kill Mountain - - - 3,190
8. High Point Mountain - - - 3.100
9. Plateau Mountain - - - - 3,855
10. Sugar Loaf and Mink Mt. - 3,807
11. Twin Mountain - - - - 3,650
12. Indian Head - - - - - 3,581
13. Overlook Mountain - - - 3,300
14. Platterkill Mountain - - - 3,200
15. Round Top - - - - - 3,500
16. Kaaterskill High Peak - - 3,800
17. Hudson River Valley - -
18. Kaaterskill Clove - - - -
19. Clum Hill - - - - - - 2,372
20. Tannersville - - - - - - 2,054
21. Mink Hollow - - - - -
22. Mount Tobias, Ulster County.
23. Stony Clove - - - - -
24. Colonel's Chair Mountain - 3,200

Boarding House Directory, 1887, Evers Collection

Thomas Nast, *Harper's Weekly*, July 21, 1866,
The Bronck Museum Collection

Catskill region retains its natural charm. The resorts tend to be clustered, leaving large stretches of enormously attractive landscape in between. While the region is compact (two hours' drive joins the two most distant points), there is lots of room and variety as you pass through the natural setting. This is in sharp contrast to the cheek-by-jowl resorts of Pennsylvania's Pocono region, which competes for vacation business with the Catskills.

Many types of Catskill resort continue to thrive, some with histories going back more than a century. The following sketches of five current Catskill resorts convey some of the flavor, texture, and complexity of the region's vacation facilities, and represent types common in Catskill development, from the old roadside inn to the cosmopolitan modern hybrid.

Five Resorts

One of the most beautiful of the inns or roadside taverns in the Catskills is Windham House in Windham. Originally built as a farmhouse by Perez Steele about 1800–1805, it was enlarged by his son, perhaps about 1840, to be one of the first local taverns where tourists could stay.

The siting of Windham House was originally determined by its use as a farm: directly across the street spread the farm fields, and a barn is close to the road. The farmhouse was ideally sited to become a roadside inn, and the farm buildings were suited to livery functions attached to the stagecoach line. Because the inn is located on a major road, it was for many years the headquarters of the Catskill & Delhi stage, which also carried the mail, and it functioned as a stagecoach hotel for commercial travelers. In 1869, a new owner enlarged the inn to serve as a boarding house with a capacity of 75 guests. The spectacular classical porch stretching all the way across the front of Windham House was added at the time; one assumes the owner regarded the verandah as essential to his establishment's new character. The classical design of the porch columns indicates a very conservative taste for 1869, but a taste in keeping with the Greek-revival architecture of numerous houses in the region.

Continuing as a vacationer's hotel, Windham House has been popular during the summer season ever since its 1869 conversion. Although the present owners have added two motel units and a cottage next door, they have reduced their capacity from seventy-five to seventy — because of the need to introduce indoor bathrooms and enlarge some of the old tiny bedrooms. In 1951, the outhouse behind the kitchen was still in use as a guest bathroom, which some found preferable to a visit to the indoor facilities up a flight of stairs. Rooms in the inn are very modest in size, and the original 9-foot ceiling height has not been changed. Solid plank construction for the old walls has made the introduction of wiring, plumbing, and heating pipes very difficult. The ground floor is open all the way across the front as a long parlor—what would have been the tavern room in early days. The dining room, which is also on the ground floor, offers a simple two choices for dinner each evening.

Meinstein's Lodge in Fleischmanns represents another Catskill tradition — the boarding house. Since many of its benefits are to be found outside its own walls—in the air, scenery, local attractions—the boarding house usually flourished where the locale was rich in interest: town life, scenic jewels, or major resort hotels which might be visited by boarders. Fleischmanns was such a town around the turn of the century—it was studded with larger hotels, had a railroad station on the resort circuit,

Meinstein's Lodge, on the main street of Fleischmanns, New York, is a modern example of the old boarding house tradition.
John Margolies, 1978

and was filled with private vacation houses and boarding houses. Its busy main street had plenty of shops and restaurants to entertain day visitors, and the nearby countryside was as graced with scenic features and fresh air and water as city dwellers could desire. A man-made lake offered a second focal point to town life.

Present-day Fleischmanns provides an image of this life in decline: more than half the hotels have closed, the railroad no longer stops there, and the main-street shops carry on only a sporadic business. The town as an intense center of resort activity has lost its energy. But Meinstein's Lodge on Main Street, fresh paint and trimmed lawns shining, insists that the place is still viable. Meinstein's is a three-building complex assembled out of three neighboring private houses. The main one, Todd House, was built in 1904 as a common-sense mansion for the wealthiest man in town. Crosby House, next door, was built in 1912. Across the street is Lorelei, constructed around 1890. When the buildings were acquired by their present owners (in 1957, 1944, and 1947, respectively), they were already in use as boarding houses for the summer trade. The three houses retain much of their original character; very few adjustments have been made to the structure—just an enlarged kitchen and dining room in one and some added bathrooms. In 1950, a set of housekeeping units was added to the property behind Todd, but otherwise it might as well be 1912.

The town of Fleishmanns has built tennis courts and a swimming pool, relieving the boarding house of the obligation to provide such facilities, but Meinstein's clientele is not especially directed toward athletics. Activities such as three meals a day and a walk down the main street are almost as satisfying now as they were for turn-of-the-century boarders; movies, quiz games, bingo, nightly piano music, and an occasional touring singer complete the diversions. While the big Fleischmanns hotels, with their nightclubs and extensive building programs, have been left behind by departing tourists, the simple boarding house thrives. Its largely German and Austrian clientele prefer its unrushed and unstylish comfort, even within dismaying sight of the abandoned successes of years gone by.

The history of Thompson House, in Windham, is a version of many resorts' histories, but more so. The resort has been in the same family for five generations, since Ira Thompson bought a farmhouse in 1880 at the urging of his friend Elbert Osborn, who had tried the boarding-house business on the farm property next door. These two houses flourished across the street from the Soper place, a converted box factory which had turned boarding house in 1866 under the name Evergreen Park House, and then The Pines. All three made use

"SOPER PLACE," CATSKILL MOUNTAINS.

The Soper Place, a boarding house in the 1860s, is one of the numerous buildings incorporated into the Thompson House complex.
Boarding House Directory, 1887, Evers Collection

of the stream that ran behind Thompson's with its dam and swimming hole. Thompson's hotel was a success, and the original building, called the Manor House, was joined by a second house nearby, called Spruce Cottage, in 1893. Herbert Thompson himself, son of the original owner, turned all the fancy woodwork on his lathe and covered the exterior with varicolored patterns of wood shingles.

Another building was added to the Thompson complex in 1950—Tamarack House—which was the first hotel facility in the area to have bedrooms with carpeting and private baths. In 1958, Thompson's put in a swimming pool and bought the old Soper place across the street. During this period, two generations of the Thompson family ran the two hotels, each with its own dining room. The 1962 addition was the Evergreen—a motel type of building and the first of the complex to have television. The major addition was made in 1968 in the form of a large dining room and kitchen building, centralizing all the food activity for the resort, and providing a large game room below and a coffee shop open to the public. In 1978 Thompson's built a theater space with tiered seating for expanded evening entertainment.

With all of this building activity, stretched out over a century, like that of some medieval cathedral, it is hardly surprising that the styles are not consistent. Instead of a unified whole, the resort presents itself as a broad survey of architectural possibilities. Public spaces at the Thompson House tend to be small, similar to domestic living spaces in scale and decoration. The lobbies in The Pines building and in the main building (erected in 1968) are broken down into living-room-size areas and furnished with chairs; Bibles are noticeable fixtures throughout. Lobbies in Spruce Cottage and Manor House are living rooms as well, and in Manor they include a piano and lots of portable chairs for entertainments. The modest bedrooms in the earliest part of the hotel conjure up nineteenth-century resort accommodations: small and equipped only with running water and closets built in to replace movable wardrobes. Narrow metal bedsteads and night tables complete the furniture in the single rooms. Bathrooms down the hall are shared, as they always were in early Catskill resorts. Large windows provide real old-fashioned ventilation. Thompson's later additions contain larger guest rooms with air conditioners, in keeping with Catskill trends.

Thompson's provides a study in the shifting value of the verandah over the years. The Manor House has a lovely long porch with extended octagonal bays at two ends and plenty of rustic furniture. From it, boarders can quietly enjoy the long sweep of lawn and trees leading down to the road and, beyond it, the golf course. Spruce Cottage next door also has a porch and a balcony on the second floor. But the motel units added in the 1960s feature large separate balconies for each unit; instead of shared verandah space, these outdoor adjuncts are compartmented off to provide privacy for each family.

The remarkable variety of the Thompson House's accommodations is united by the force of its family personality rather than by any visual unity. And, as is typical of the smaller Catskill hotels, no attempt has been made to physically link the separate buildings of the complex. The various houses and additions sit comfortably near one another with well-kept lawns, trees, pool, and an 1880 summer house among them, and no one feels that weather-protected linkages are desirable. For the Thompsons, being out of doors is an important part of being there, not something to be guarded against.

Part of the special character of the Thompson House comes from its choice not to serve alcohol. A roadhouse-restaurant not far down the road satisfies the wayward appetite, but no bar is part of Thompson's architecture, nor is there nightclub, ballroom, or even dance floor. Parlors are the meeting places for the evening crowd who gather after dinner to create their own entertainment—usually attending to the contributions of a particularly musical guest playing the piano. Now the new theater adds movies and concerts to the evening offerings.

The Thompson family is its own architect, builder, and decorator—a not unusual phenomenon in family-owned hotels. Family members entertain guests during their season — mid-May to mid-October—and spend the cooler months making repairs and additions. They have always used their own labor in all areas of the business, feeling a closer link with their guests through their participation and sustaining the image of home through all their expansions.

At the Mohonk Mountain House in New Paltz, siting and landscape gardening have been combined for an excellent version of the nineteenth century picturesque. The glacial lake site, originally occupied by a small tavern before purchase by the Smiley family in 1870, is naturally dramatic because of the abrupt rock cliffs which frame the water. These cliffs, however, are domestically scaled, so the impression of wild sublimity is tempered by the landscape's easily apprehensible size. The Smileys, always interested in conservation and natural improvement, spent years bringing in topsoil and introducing lawns and more formal gardens to their mountain, which add to the paradoxical tranquility of the glacial scar. More ambitious than most hotels in developing the potential in landscape, Mohonk has laid out miles of bridle trails (used in winter for cross-country skiing) through five thousand acres of forest — much of which is now owned by the Mohonk Trust, a device for protecting the land from development while preserving it from taxes. In picturesque English-garden style, these trails lead to viewing points where certain peaks, valleys, and rock formations can be seen to best advantage.

The memorable architecture of Mohonk is a collection of the styles popular between 1870 and 1903, when the resort building reached its present, and since then stable, form. Buildings, additions, and replacements for outmoded parts join together in a long, irregular line along the edge of a rock-bordered lake to form the hotel. Wood meets stone, shingle shifts to tile, browns and grays give way to greens and reds — creating either a disturbing eclecticism or an enchantingly varied romantic fantasy, depending on the eye of the beholder. Because of its being built in pieces, Mohonk differs from the more unified but now lost monuments of the railroad era, but its size and scale are similar, and it has the same attentive relation to its site.

Public space at Mohonk is centered in the parlor addition, constructed in 1900 according to James Ware's "Tyrolean" design. Here a wonderful two-story main room provides meeting space for concerts, lectures, or just sitting. Corners of the grand-scale room are separated by railings, and built-in seating creates intimate bays for close conversation. On the floor below is a second parlor with a lower ceiling; each is surrounded on three sides with porches that hang over the lake. The parlor wing is itself a bridge spanning a bit of lake to better integrate the site into the guests' experience. The Mohonk dining room, added in 1891–92 by Napoleon LeBrun and Sons, is, like the parlor, a sensitive display of woodworking in the arts-and-crafts spirit of the late nineteenth century. The end of the dining room bows out toward a spectacular view of valley and Catskill Mountains; picture windows are genuinely serviceable here, complemented by a clerestory. These two light-filled rooms are unique in the Catskills, where design, for the most part, is not aesthetically memorable.

The Mohonk bedroom, generous in size at an average 12 × 20 feet, retains a flavor of simpler times. It has no air conditioning, only the cool

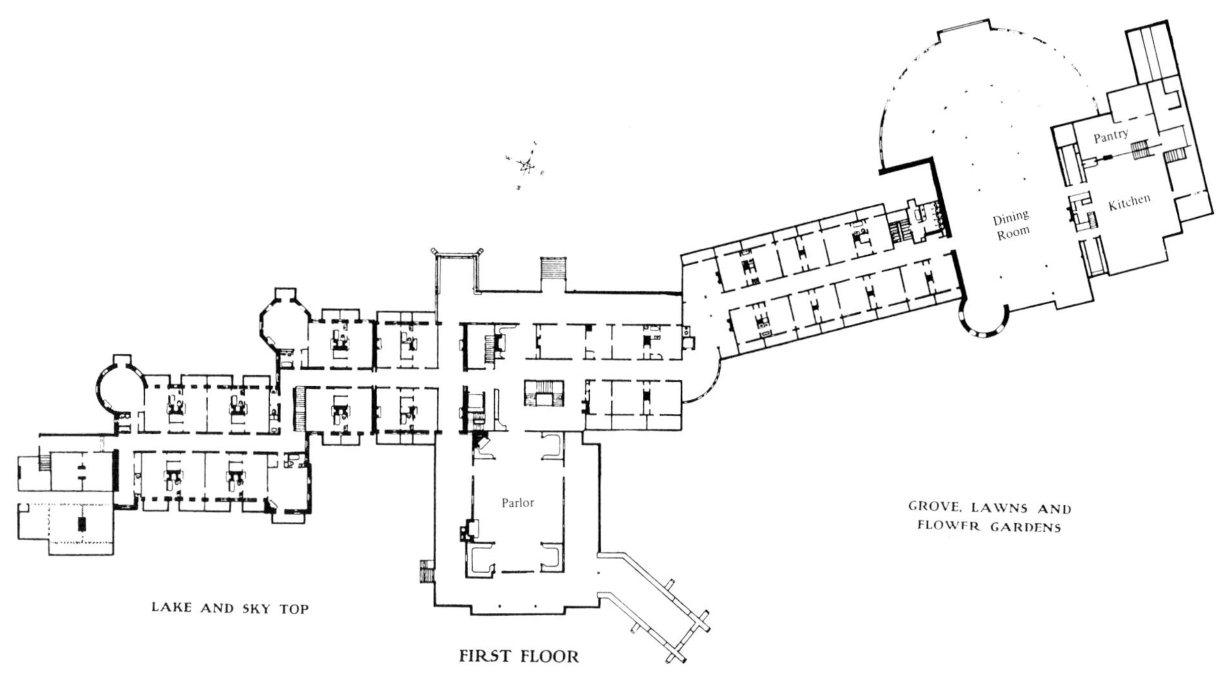

The 1910 Mohonk plan shows a hallway that extends from one end of the building to the other. Its offsets and jogs prevent the boredom of an "endless" corridor. Mohonk Mountain House, New Paltz, New York

breezes of its carefully chosen setting. While the house is heated, most rooms also feature fireplaces for cool fall or freezing winter evenings. Furniture is simple — a straight chair, an oak desk, a plain wooden bedstead, a rug. Bathrooms have been introduced into almost all the bedrooms now, at the sacrifice of some of the smaller bedrooms. Sometimes this has been a matter of turning three early bedrooms into two modern-size rooms with baths and closets; while this means a serious loss of income-producing rooms, rooms without baths are not likely to attract many guests these days.

Mohonk bedrooms all have balconies, and such are the treasures of the site that both sides of the building offer splendid views — a scenic valley and mountains on one side and the glacial lake with its miniature cliffs on the other. The wide, tall hallways on the bedroom floors are spacious enough to encourage ventilating breezes. And the halls jog, turn, or shift axis often enough (because of the additive, three-decade building process) to make progress through them interesting: at each jog, the hallways widen into sitting areas with a set of windows and some scenic views framed on the walls — a surprise parlor instead of a mere corridor.

The Homowack, a Sullivan County giant in Spring Glen, provides a classic example of the development of southern Catskill hotels. In 1922 the Fatt family, Polish immigrants migrating again from New York City, bought a dairy farm and opened the farmhouse to summer boarders. Additional guest quarters were built, and the establishment went by the name of "Fatt's Cottages." Renamed Homowack Lodge — from the Indian term for the town — in 1925, the early facilities amounted to the original 17-room house and a second house containing the dining room. Fatt's five children helped out, and home-grown entertainment such as mock marriages filled the guests' needs for diversion.

Homowack's present manager, Irv Blickstein, ran a lumberyard in nearby Ellenville during the 1930s, supplying building materials to several hotels. During the Depression years the hotels tended to be slow in paying their bills. When Blickstein married Florence Fatt, the daughter of Homowack, he believed the hotel business had little to recommend it. But efforts to sell Homowack Lodge failed, and by 1940 Blickstein could not give it away. Persisting through difficult times, he was more than ready for the post–World War II boom, and around 1946 he added his first new building: 13 rooms and an indoor swimming pool. Blickstein continued expanding through 1972. From the original 17-room farmhouse, Homowack grew to 320 guest rooms with private baths, an immense nightclub, separate swimming pools and dining rooms for children and adults, indoor and outdoor tennis courts, and a children's recreation hall, as well as the usual card and game rooms, beauty salon, health club, and lobbies and meeting rooms. Today Homowack can sustain a capacity crowd of about nine hundred guests.

Characteristically, the growth of Homowack has resulted in impressive horizontal spread, decreasing emphasis on site and view, and an increase in private luxury in guest rooms. Additions to the hotel have maintained a two- to three-story height

The Homowack in Spring Glen is comprised of buildings erected between 1946 and 1972. John Margolies, 1978

in wings which branch out from the focal main lobby and dining-room building. The elevators in the new wings are intended primarily to facilitate the transportation of luggage, rather than to make additional height possible. These branching wings connect to earlier wings, and continuous passageways internally link all parts of the hotel—but the trip from a newer guest room to the nightclub in a central older building can be so tortuous that one would rather go outside and re-enter through the main lobby than wend one's way through the backstairs labyrinth. This route is outrageous enough to provide subject matter for Homowack's nightclub comics.

The most recently built guest rooms in the Homowack's Paradise Wing, opened in 1972, offer dimensions of about 28 × 25 feet, plus bathrooms with Japanese-inspired custom-made tiled bathtubs the size of small swimming pools — in themselves worth the trip. Two queen-size beds, wall-to-wall carpet, and the white noise of air conditioning make each room as comfortable and quiet as modern guests can imagine. That the picture windows look out on other picture windows is not particularly noticeable when the drapes are drawn. The plush bedrooms are rather unceremoniously strung along both sides of dark, minimally decorated corridors, narrow and infinitely extended; the transition from public circulation to private room is a change from the legal minimum to the lap of luxury.

Because Homowack began as a resort during the

Kutsher's 1930s building, with its modern 1950s entrance lobby addition, epitomizes the disjunctive styles in Catskill transformations. Kutsher's Country Club, Monticello, New York

automobile era, issues of siting tended to be reduced only to the question of access by car. The landscape in which the hotel is set is of minor importance; landscaping around the buildings is also minimal, as well-kept lawns merge into golf-course greens. The building, unassertively modern in style, makes no gesture toward the landscape; its glass and concrete surfaces ignore the textures and colors of surrounding nature. The building seems not to have been designed to be seen as a whole, but rather to be perceived only piece by piece, and even then, principally from the interior. It is easy to come away with an image of "the nightclub," "the dining room," or "the bedroom," rather than any sense of how the parts work together. This is because the location of additions was always more dependent on available land and on the nondisruption of continuing hotel life than it was on ideal spatial or formal relationships.

Architectural Diversity

As these five portraits demonstrate, the Catskill resort as an architectural type has no consistent form. The kinds of buildings enlisted or constructed for the resorts range from the old wooden farmhouse to the huge steel, concrete, and glass high-rise complex. But whether they consist of former roadside inns, hotel blocks built for the purpose of taking one or two hundred vacationers, or motels and bungalow colonies, by far the most common resort is a composite of some or even all of these physical types.

The only consistency among resorts is in their additive development and in the speed with which they have changed. Most resorts began small and added facilities when the need arose. Hotel owners are also the original recyclers, adapting existing buildings to new uses. And so the typical Catskill resort is a set of parts done in different styles and materials for different purposes, with no inherent unity of design, and often no unity imposed after the fact either. The hotel that remains in its original form might even be considered a failure, having been unable to add the facilities required in modern times.

No other kind of architecture undergoes such continuous adaptation. The necessity for it is forced on the resort from two directions. The constant use and wear of the buildings is exaggerated in hotels by the rapid turnover in guests. People use up the rugs, wall coverings, roadways, lawns, and china at an astounding rate. Artifacts from earlier hotel days are missing today simply because they have been consumed.

From the other side, hotels must constantly add a little something to attract guests. Up-to-date conveniences and comforts are always needed to make the resort competitive. And so it is that indoor plumbing destroys the original layout of the Greek-revival tavern, fire-code gypsum board encloses the Victorian stair, and nylon carpets the dining-room parquet. Along with the gains come the losses. Were hotel owners to maintain historical purity in the forms and surfaces of their hotels, they would soon be out of business. Many period carcasses dot the hillsides today, succumbing to weeds and waiting for fire.

Catskill resort architecture is so eager to reuse, add on, and modernize that it makes a particularly poor subject for analysis with the usual tools of architectural history. Indeed, architects have little place in this story. Most resort work of the past was done by builders who worked out designs with hotel owners, who themselves were inspired by the suggestions of their patrons. Catskill hotels were built in most of the styles currently fashionable in larger American culture: Greek-revival, Queen Anne, and shingle style are all in evidence. But Catskill builders were seldom innovators of architectural style; they simply used what was available, making adjustments of their own to suit local needs.

Catskill builders were not innovators in building technology either, and developments in steel and concrete construction were slow to be adopted there. Elevators were rarely used in nineteenth-century Catskill resorts, although urban hotels found them essential; luggage hoists helped the staff to manage travelers' trunks, and the four-story height of most resort hotels was a short enough climb. Central heating was also a latecomer to the Catskills, usually because the resorts did not stay open all year and fireplaces sufficed for spring and fall heat. The sole interest resort owners had in technology was in the realm of gadgets: the telephone had appeared in the Catskill resorts by 1879, telegraph connections were always offered by the larger nineteenth-century houses, and contemporary hotels find extravagant inventions such as the artificial-snow maker and the Jacuzzi whirlpool-bath attachment are very attractive to tourists.

Aesthetic quality must be bypassed because making such judgments requires treating each building as an object and judging its architectural refinements. Instead, the building must be regarded as an interplay between physical object, user, site, and time. Any resort today is not a final result but a moment in passage of an ever changing architectural event.

What makes Catskill resort architecture comprehensible after abandoning the usual stylistic and aesthetic criteria is a set of themes that organize observations regardless of a building's size, date, or style. The first theme is siting — how the resort is placed in relation to the natural and man-made landscapes. A related theme is the transitional space that partakes of both outdoors and in — the verandah and the gazebo. Another theme is planning, which focuses the view of the organization of parts in the resort to see how spatial relationships have altered over time. Finally, there is the theme of public/private spatial order; entertainment rooms, the dining room, and the lobby are major public interior spaces found in nearly every resort. The private bedroom is also a universal element which may be studied as it changes over time.

Isolating these themes provides an opportunity to analyze trends and to show the direction of development in Catskill resort architecture. This development, we suggest, begins with an outward-directed architecture responsive to the natural landscape and turns into an inward-directed architecture responsive to the social landscape.

But trends in resorts are noticeable only at those particular places that concern themselves with change and modernity. The other ongoing Catskill resorts allow the needs of the present to be met with qualities of siting, planning, and public or private space that were new only at some time in the past.

Siting

The first tourist hotel in the Catskills, the 1823 Catskill Mountain House, was sited close to the Hudson River, on a cliff overlooking the Hudson Valley and points east. From its position above the world, the hotel accommodated those Romantics who wanted a sense of the vastness and wildness of nature, tempered by the contributions of civilization. Every village, steeple, and road of the Hudson Valley was on display from the hotel's vantage point.

In the railroad era following the Civil War, hotels were sited with an eye to waterfalls, impressive mountains, hiking trails, and panoramic views. Advertisements of the era stressed these characteristics: "The view of the mountains and the valley from the broad piazzas of the Grand is superb indeed . . . you get a magnificent panorama." The Prospect Park Hotel offered "the finest and most varied scenery of any house in America. Views in five states." One finds in 1870s advertising an equal

Arts and Crafts meets Art Deco in the Sugar Maples lobby, c. 1940. Sugar Maples, Maplecrest, New York

The 1823 Mountain House was the first resort hotel in the region: "...Its appearance is very much that of a small white cloud in the midst of the heavens, and it is in the highest degree wild and romantic. But I came to the conclusion, after gazing at it a considerable time, that the fatigue of climbing to the summit...would be infinitely greater than the pleasure its airy situation could afford." Anonymous account, 1829, in *New York State Tradition,* 1867. Thomas Nast, *Harper's Weekly,* July 21, 1866, The Bronck Museum Collection

emphasis on natural beauties and ease of access, with certain hotels claiming that a trip up to a mountaintop was so wearying that the view was hardly worth it and that true vacation pleasure meant staying in the comfortable valley below—near the railroad station. In 1881, Tremper House advertised, "It is the only house in the Catskills that can be reached without a long and tedious stage or wagon ride, *being within sight* of the railroad station."

Only slightly less important than the view from the hotel was the addition the hotel itself made to the view. The best way to promote the hotel was to site it and advertise it as a picturesque enhancement of the locale: "The pleasing outline of the Summit Mountain as it appears against the sky... reminds one of some charming picture. The elegant and palatial work of art so near its crest [The Grand Hotel], apparently embedded in the virgin forest, is a prominent feature in the landscape...."

Hotels advertising in the 1880s and 1890s did not hesitate to feature other hotels as part of the attractive view. The Maple Grove House invited tourists to take in the "splendid view of the mountains and the

UNRIVALED SUMMER RESORT.

PROSPECT PARK HOTEL,

CATSKILL, N. Y.

Season of 1887—June 1st to October 15th.

THIS LARGE AND ELEGANT HOUSE is situated on a high cliff in the centre of an extensive wooded park, commanding the finest and most varied scenery of any house in America. Views in five States. Salubrious mountain air. Shaded walks and drives. Spacious parlors and dining hall. The grandest piazza in this country. Strictly first-class. Very accessible. The most central and convenient house for families who desire to visit the many places of interest. Terms unusually moderate. The difference as compared with other first-class summer hotels will pay a family's extra expenses in visiting the various attractive points.

The amusements are—Pleasant Walks and Drives, Boating, Fishing, Bowling, Billiards, Croquet, Lawn Tennis, Roller Skating and Dancing. A First-Class Orchestra. Good Livery and Boarding Stables.

Boarding House Directory, 1887, Evers Collection

"It is the only house in the Catskills that can be reached without a long and tedious stage or wagon ride, *being within sight of the railroad station.*" Tremper House advertisement, *Ulster & Delaware Guide,* 1881. *Boarding House Directory,* 1887, Evers Collection

Mountain House" while the Drummond Falls House commanded "fine views of Kaaterskill Clove, Overlook Mountain, Mountain House, etc., from the extensive piazza." The Catskill Mountain House was treated, like a mountain peak or waterfall, as a dramatic element of Catskill scenery.

By the early twentieth century, people's taste for wilderness began to diversify into an appreciation of a broader and varied range of scenery, and hotels were able to succeed in all kinds of settings. In the Catskills, ragged cliffs or rolling hills are only a few miles apart; rivers and waterfalls in the northern

"**BEAUTIFUL FOR SITUATION.**"

The views from the porch of THE NEW GRAND HOTEL are the most attractive in the whole Catskill Range and include The Slide, 4,220 feet, the highest point of all the Catskills.

THE GRAND HOTEL (IN THE HEART OF THE CATSKILLS).

Parlor Cars to the Lawn of the Hotel *via* West Shore and Ulster & Delaware Railroad.

Rates, $4.50 per Day, *Address, HARVEY S. DENISON, Summit Mountain Post-office, Ulster County, N. Y.*

Boarding House Directory, 1887, Evers Collection

THE HOTEL OF THE CATSKILLS.

HOTEL KAATERSKILL,

3,000 FEET ABOVE THE LEVEL OF THE SEA.

NINETY MILES OF HUDSON RIVER VALLEY IN SIGHT.

LARGEST MOUNTAIN HOUSE IN THE WORLD.

DIRECT ACCESS BY RAIL NOW COMPLETED.

FULL BAND OF MUSIC, SIXTEEN PERFORMERS.

PERFECT ORGANIZATION AND CUISINE.

THIRTY MILES OF DRIVES, TWENTY MILES OF WOODED WALKS.

Beautiful Lakes, Waterfalls, Extensive Livery, Large Ball-room, Rooms *en suite*, Baths, every modern convenience.

OPEN UNTIL OCTOBER 1, 1887.

W. F. PAIGE, Manager,

KAATERSKILL P. O., GREENE, CO. N. Y.

Boarding House Directory, 1887, Evers Collection

Nast's drawing of the piazza or verandah, the *sine qua non* of Catskill resorts. Thomas Nast, *Harper's Weekly*, July 21, 1866, The Bronck Museum Collection

areas have their counterparts in the lakes and more gentle scenery of the southern section. With the advent of the automobile after 1900, a choice of transportation modes gave latitude to the siting of hotels, while road building made previously hard-to-reach sites more attractive to developers.

The resort town of Stamford, for example, promoted both its observation tower — built by Utsayantha Mountain Club, from which you could see twenty-eight Catskill peaks, the Berkshires, the Adirondacks, and the Green Mountains — and the decorous "flagged walks and maple trees . . . [and] well kept lawns" of the hotels in town. The new tourist wanted clean air and fresh food and water and did not require sublimity so much as hospitality.

Over the years, the hotels' emphasis has tipped from siting themselves in relation to nature's spectacle to creating their own spectacle with a rather incidental relation to site. Where in the past being in the country was the very point of going to the Catskills, at the modern hotel the country setting is simply a backdrop for social activities.

Nevertheless, being in the country is still crucial for the modern resort. Even in the grandest of large-scale Sullivan County places, where much of the environment is air-conditioned and weatherproofed, guests still prefer the outdoor pool and the genuine suntan. Even if they never need experience the sultry summer — thanks to individual room air conditioners — they are still heliotropic enough to care if the sun is out. And even if dining rooms and nightclubs are now sometimes built without windows, one still views the natural backdrop as essential to one's promenade to and from these social centers. The trees and bushes outside the plate-glass corridors are as critical for a sense of place as the corridors themselves. Nature has not at all been abandoned, it has simply been reframed.

Hotel owners have always complemented the natural attributes of their sites with man-made landscaped environments. The owners of the Mountain House on its clifftop site created a lawn from the verandah down to the cliff edge and also introduced vegetable gardens. The Grand Hotel was set on a "gently sloping lawn" which gave way to forest. The Kaaterskill's surrounding woods, which it called "a princely park of nearly 21 square miles of mountain and valley," were laced with riding trails and carriage drives. At the Rexmere in Stamford, a large park with an allée of trees was laid out at the turn of the century by Frederick Law Olmsted, Jr. Equally ambitious was the extensive landscaping done around Mohonk Mountain House.

For the most part, Catskill landscape gardening sticks to the "natural" idiom of Olmsted and the English-garden tradition, where the winding path opens out onto the view as if by surprise. Occasionally one finds something more exotic, such as the Japanese garden at Yama Farms in Ellenville, but that is the exception. Formal symmetrical landscape gardens are also rare, although certainly elements of formality can be found in Rexmere's allée or in the bedded plants and flowers at Mohonk or the Concord. For practical reasons, Catskill landscape gardeners put most of their efforts into creating a lawn: it served as a pretty setting for the buildings and doubled as the arena for several sports.

The Verandah

From the first, the expansive porch, piazza, or verandah was an important feature; indeed, it was the very mark of a resort hotel. Both in-town inns and country hotels had their verandahs: at once part of the outdoors and part of the indoors, they were places where guests could appreciate nature without really having to be in it. Throughout the nineteenth century, no matter what the stylistic intentions of a hotel's design, it had to have a verandah, and no resort from Saratoga to Cape May got along without one.

The verandah was built on the side of the hotel that had the best view. At the Grand Hotel on Summit Mountain in 1881, "Guests enter the building from the rear, and, passing across the spacious Rotunda, gain access to the broad and lengthy piazza, 110 feet of which is twenty feet wide, where the wonderful mountain and valley view bursts upon them with astonishment."

Supplied with broad steps and rocking chairs, the verandah was the place to wait, to have one's picture taken, to meet other guests, to start off from, to return to. It was a place to watch lawn sports, to gossip and court. It was a little stage, a theater of resort life.

It was an architectural theater too. The most ornamental details of carpentry were lavished on the verandah, distinguishing it as the architectural showplace of the whole building. Double-decker verandahs were common for early inns in the Catskills, and it is easy to imagine that they acted as signboards to announce the presence of a lodging place. The porch on such a building often had columns that rose a full two stories, and sometimes even three or four. A second-floor porch might extend all the way out to the columnar front or be held back and supported on brackets—like a balcony within the enclosure of the verandah. Such porches on in-town inns usually fronted on the street, and sometimes they wrapped around two sides of the building. In country resorts, verandahs occasionally expanded to wrap around the entire building, but more often they stayed on the front.

The verandah's sources are to be found in its function as exterior circulation space. In order to save precious interior space and money, builders sometimes made outdoor halls and stairs instead

An elaborate three-level verandah wraps around the street façades of the Olcott House in Wurtsboro, c. 1870. Manville Wakefield Collection

of providing for interior circulation. Structures as different as the Roman atrium house or the bungalow of India have historically made use of an extended roof to shelter exterior passages which link one room of a house to another. The inns of seventeenth-century England also used this device.

Architectural historian Niklaus Pevsner identified the full-blown verandah specifically with the American resort hotel. As one of the earliest examples, he cited the 1812 Congress Hotel in Cape May on the New Jersey shore. It featured an impressive verandah, no longer for economical circulation but as a space of its own, mediating between outdoors and indoors. The development may have come about as a function of climate; interior rather than exterior circulation was needed in colder climates than those of Rome or India. But the change may also reflect the influence of resort guests in shaping the new use of the verandah. Proprietors and guests discussed hotel verandahs in terms of length: the porch increased in value as it increased in feet. Smart tourists knew how many laps around the verandah equaled a mile, so the day's constitutional could be taken on the porch if the weather was bad. In the 1920s, hotels advertised their verandah sizes in square feet to seem more grandiose.

In the Flagler, the original Concord, and other new resort buildings of the twenties, a glassed-in ground floor supplanted, or sometimes merely supplemented, the old verandah. The resulting enclosed porch provided views and a connection with nature similar to the earlier version, but it added more protection from the elements. The result was a domesticated verandah experience, turned inward into the hotel's controlling atmosphere, less at the mercy of weather and insects but also less intimate with the landscape.

In the 1920s, protected glassed-in porches with rattan furniture and plants preserved the outdoor feeling of the verandah. Sun room, "New Flagler" Hotel, Fallsburg, New York, 1920. Manville Wakefield Collection

This trend of glassing-in anticipated today's use of long glass-walled corridors to link the many separate buildings of a resort complex into one system (Kutsher's, Brown's, or the Stevensville in Sullivan County). These modern glass corridors may include sitting spaces as well as circulation routes: Grossinger's parlor-corridor is appropriately called "the Verandah." Where early verandahs remain at the large modern hotels, they exist as relics of a time when the rocking chair was host to a very different style of vacationer.

Recent variants on outdoor verandahs can be seen in Haines Falls. At the Rosa del Monte, the nineteenth-century two-story verandah has been extended on its lower level to become a redwood deck, furnished with tables and chairs for outdoor dining. Part of the deck is roofed by the upper floor of the old verandah, and part is open to the sky. An earlier hotel expansion in the form of a perpendicular wing had made the house into an **L** around the verandah, so the new deck is very comfortably nestled in the crook of the house.

Another version of the verandah occurs a block away, at the Villa Maria. Various remodeling jobs have shortened the old verandah to perhaps a third of its original length, but the space has been more than replaced by a paved piazza, closely akin to its Italian namesake. Now the Villa Maria's piazza space fills in between the street and the façade of the hotel, and events on the street become part of the resort action. At its rear, away from the street, the Villa Maria offers a pool, a boccie court, Ping-Pong, and other activities. But unlike Brown's, for example, where such amusements lure everyone away from the street, in Haines Falls the street still retains its interest, and a place is provided — expanding upon the old verandah space and use — to enjoy it.

The gazebo or summer house is an offspring of the verandah—like a little segment of a front porch freestanding in nature. It has all the qualities of a civilized outpost, a place to rest and watch the natural and social spectacle. As a creation of culture placed in nature, it also suggests protection against the raw and the untamed. The phenomenon of the gazebo as a protected place is especially evident at Mohonk. There gazebos are spotted along a glacial rock path on which enormous boulders seem to be in arrested motion. Amid these powerful crags, the gazebos offer metaphorical safety. At the same time, their weathered and giddy stance on each precipice adds a romantic gloss to the view: see how the frail works of man stack up against eternity!

Some resorts play it safe and keep the summer house right on the front lawn, only a short putt from its parent verandah. These summer houses serve mainly as ornaments for the hotel, and they lack the advantages of a specialized view. Such a domesticated gazebo may find its modern counterpart in the beach umbrella, which both stakes out space and protects from the sun.

The modern equivalent of the verandah is the poolside patio. Pools are often sited within the embrace of hotel wings and overlooked by decks and terraces. There the chaise longue rests from its victory over the rocking chair, and the vacationer from his encounter with lunch. The view of mountain peaks is supplanted by the view of fellow tourists. Spatially, the hotel poolside works like a suburban backyard. Where the urban house-dweller faces the street and the neighborhood, his suburban counterpart faces the private backyard, insisting on the separateness of his own family group. We have seen that the modern trend to increased privacy affects the resort "family" too. Many of today's resorts turn their backs on region and town, put up fences, and abandon the outward-directed view from the verandah.

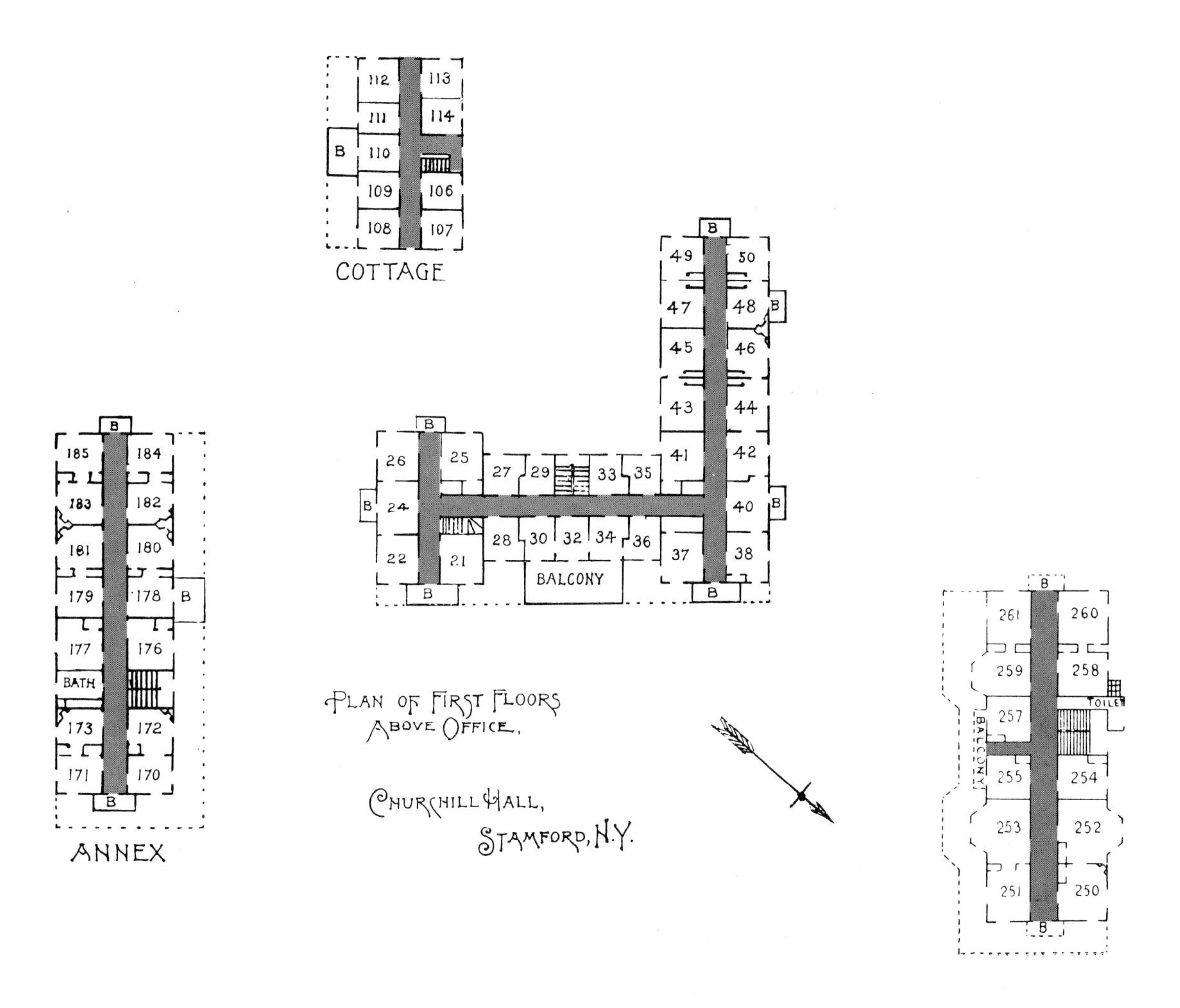

Simple rectilinear buildings have rooms opening off both sides of central corridors (shown darkened). These four buildings together comprise Churchill Hall, c. 1905. Churchill Hall, Stamford, New York, undated brochure, Evers Collection

Planning

Catskill resort planning—that is, room organization and the relationships of functional spaces to each other—is as inconsistent and varied as the building types used for resorts. Hotels which began as a single building are confronted with establishing new spatial relationships every time they need to expand. Nevertheless, there are some interesting themes in resort planning that lend some order to the variety. In general we find that the earliest hotel is one building extended by wings. When prosperity requires new facilities, they are added in the form of separate buildings on the site, only to be united again under one modern roof.

The old standard hotel block holding one hundred or so guests tends to look like a long bar, three or four stories high. At first, when additional space was needed, wings were added which duplicated the plan of the original. Here the standard plan for guest-room floors was the straightforward double-loaded corridor, with the hall down the center and rooms opening off both sides. A simple scheme that provided every room with a window to the exterior (which presumably meant a view), it also facilitated the creation of suites, when the occasion warranted, by opening up contiguous rooms along one side of the corridor. The corridors usually ended in a window which supplied both light and ventilation and served as a fire escape.

In hotels built according to this plan, there are very few corner rooms with opposed windows and consequent cross-ventilation. Given their rarity, corner rooms were always in high demand and could fetch high prices. The demand was so annoying to one hotel owner that in the 1960s he had his new guest wings designed with no corner rooms—every room has windows only on one wall—in order to forestall guests' pleas for switching accommodations. Air conditioning has now made the desire for cross-ventilation seem old-fashioned, but the prestige of the corner room lingers on.

More than wings were needed for hotel expansion. It is hard to find a Catskill resort that does not have at least a few separate outbuildings. In the later nineteenth century, hotels advertised separate buildings for billiards and bowling; during the 1920s these recreation buildings evolved into the more social casino, usually featuring a dance floor. Many resorts today still have their game rooms and evening's entertainment in a detached casino building in order to isolate the noise from sleeping areas, and to give the guests a feeling of going somewhere special. At the Villa Maria, the casino building is only 100 feet from the lobby, but one makes a special trip outdoors to get there; at Gavin's Golden Hill in East Durham, the nightclub is actually attached to the main building, but the entrance is separate, and one goes outdoors and downhill to reach it. Getting there becomes an event. Because the entertainment is meant to attract the public as well as the hotel guests, it is desirable that the nightclub seem independent from the site of other hotel activities.

Detached guest-room units are another common feature of resort structures. The expansion of sleeping quarters seems to be an almost continual activity for the successful resort. In simpler times, hotels simply put up tents on the lawn for their overflow guests, or set up cots on the verandah. Constant need for more rooms encouraged making the tent solution permanent, in the form of little cottages near the main buildings.

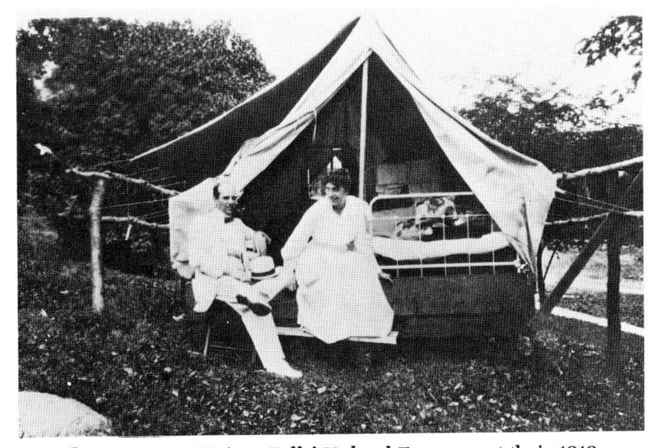

Overflow guests at Haines Falls' Upland Farm spent their 1919 vacations in tents. The more prosperous hotels made such provisions permanent in the form of cottages or bungalows. Haines Falls Free Library Collection

The 1879 Tremper House and its grounds in Shandaken "contain not only the large hotel and its accessory buildings, but also several detached cottages for the greater convenience of family parties who desire a measure of privacy with the advantages of a large hotel." The main hotel building acted as a focus and social center for guests who might sleep in separate cottages. Twilight Park, a private vacation community in Haines Falls, also ordered the social life of individual vacation households around its own hotels.

Separate guest bungalows flourished during the "camp" era of the 1930s and 1940s. A batch of friends arriving together at a resort could share a cottage and enjoy their group privacy, yet still be part of all the activity. The railroad guidebooks promoted bungalows as a strong selling point for the resorts: the White Roe at Livingston Manor advertised "a new contingent of deluxe bungalettes, each with private shower and luxuriously furnished." The Shawanga Lodge had "cozy and picturesque bungalows and cottages." Camp Livingston, an adult camp in Livingston Manor, housed guests in the "luxurious hotel (with or without bath) and in cottages. . . . The Lake Shore Bungalows are exceedingly pretty and provide hotel comforts, including electric lights, hot and cold showers, in-built wardrobes, dressers."

Guest-room adjuncts in the form of small cottages arranged in a **U** were popular at the Hotel Brickman during the great singles era of the thirties and forties. Archly designated "College Campus," they were built in 1933, with each six-bedroom bungalow bearing the name of a college. Rooms were tiny, but they sufficed for the groups of men and women who saw the resort as simply an arena in which to meet members of the opposite sex, and did not spend much time indoors. When they were converted to modern needs, it took six of the original rooms to comprise two of the new ones, another indication of the steady march toward more generous spatial expectations. Today the cottages are all linked with the main building by continuous walkways, and it is only from the rear that one might guess they were once separate houses.

Contemporary with this bedroom-outbuilding period was the development of the resort bungalow colony, which prevailed as an inexpensive vacation alternative throughout the middle twentieth century and is still common today. The bungalows were small cottages which accommodated one to four families each, sometimes with their own cooking facilities, but often with central kitchens to be shared. Instead of being adjuncts to a bigger resort complex, bungalows constituted a resort in themselves, independent of any "main" hotel building. They were often fairly primitive: the continued advertising of electric light up through World War II makes one suspect a reluctance on the part of Catskill bungalow owners to partake of the fruits of technology.

The related "kochelein," another low-budget vacation option, is a resort term specific about only one thing: cooking. A farmhouse, a private house converted for the purpose, or some set of small buildings—all can qualify if the kitchen is set up so that each family staying there is assigned a portion of a stove, a shelf for pots and pans, and a fraction of the refrigerator. The delegation of territory

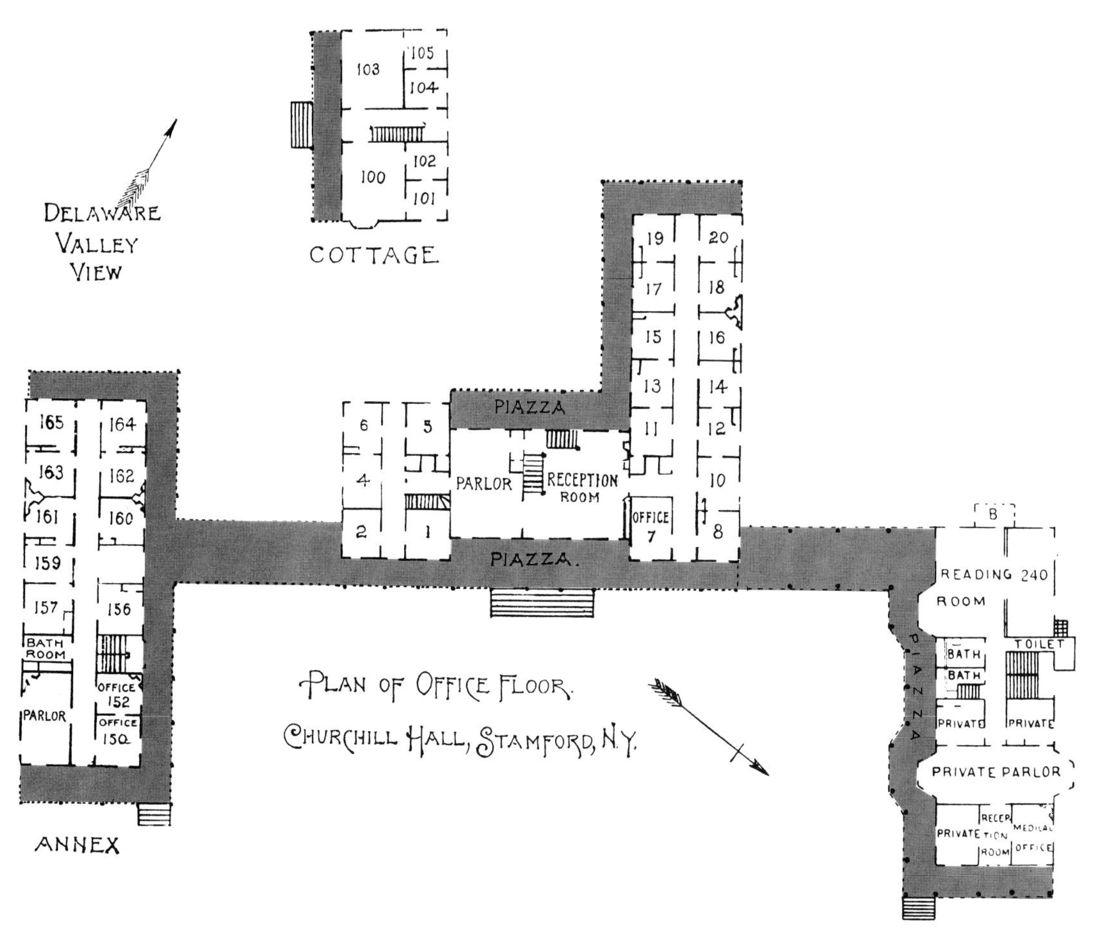

Churchill Hall's verandah (shown darkened) links three parts of the hotel. Illustrations from period guidebooks record the hotel's growth from two buildings in 1887 to three in 1903. Churchill Hall, Stamford, New York, undated brochure and *Boarding House Directory*, 1887, Evers Collection

within the building was rigidly defined and tenaciously held, but no specific architectural form developed to match this social organization.

Still another kind of building which came to qualify as a resort structure is the motel, more interesting in the Catskills as an addition to existing hotels than as a type of its own. Developed on the heels of the automobile, perhaps as early as the late teens, and certainly by the 1920s, the motel was an American west-coast invention modeled on ranch buildings, which themselves came out of the Spanish tradition of the southwest. The principal features of the motel were its horizontal expansion, one room deep, with access from a porch, and the fact that no internal circulation offered communication from room to room. Economical to build, the motel had an up-to-the-minute flavor for hotels wishing to be perceived as modern; its individual entrances also offered a certain aura of independence to the clientele, placing the motel on a privacy scale halfway between an individual cottage and a hotel. With its associations with the open road, however, the motel is really antithetical to the resort hotel's desire to be all-satisfying; by its very name, it conjures up dreams of moving on rather than the feelings of permanence which resorts seek to foster in their guests.

When the Brickman built its motel unit in 1949, it was named the Ranch House, after the western examples which the owner had seen during his wartime travels. In keeping with its sources, the Brickman motel was covered in smooth stucco with arches and an extended roof that recalled the Spanish-influenced western ranch houses. When the Villa Roma added its motel units, it was more for the sake of economy than style and because they could easily be extended—first by horizontal additions, then by adding another floor on top of the first. The several motel units added to the Sugar Maples in Maplecrest over the last twenty years are loosely disposed over the grounds along with the no less than forty other buildings of various ages that constitute the resort. These include about a dozen private homes that have been absorbed into the complex, making the resort seem remarkably like a small town.

Linkages between individual buildings of the Catskill resort are now commonplace, and, in the larger places, they are the very sign of modernity. By now the linkages have their own tradition, and they are, in a sense, a continuation of the original function of the verandah as a circulation space. When hotels expanded their facilities, open links were built to join one part to another and to protect clientele from the weather. A good example is Churchill Hall in Stamford, whose main building was erected in 1883. A second unit was built next to the first in 1887, and the addition formed one side of a **U** with the original block. By 1903, the complementary side of the **U** had been added, also as a separate building—all three had their own verandahs—and the three had been linked with covered columned walkways joining the space of the verandahs to each other. This complex added up to "600 [feet] of broad piazza."

Today's linking passages take various forms. One practical solution is the Nevele's underground passageways that link all the buildings containing guest rooms to the dining room and main lobby area. Of course, being invisible from the outside, these corridors are unable to advertise themselves as the latest modern feature. More common is the tentaclelike glass corridor of the Stevensville, an aboveground linking of buildings erected at various times, through which guests are forced to follow some tortuous routes.

Since the openings of the first big Catskill hotels, one of the standard if unmentionable features of the architecture has been the endless corridor. Plans of nineteenth-century hotels like the Grand confirm that endlessness is hardly a modern invention, although some of the larger Sullivan County resorts have developed the theme to even greater lengths than their nineteenth-century predecessors. Here is manifested one of the eternal conflicts of resort design: the buildings should be at one with nature, but the clientele would prefer a little less intimacy with the landscape than that. Thus the buildings spread horizontally and keep a low profile for fear of disrupting the scenery, but the horizontal spread increases travel time between different functional areas. Weather permitting, one can always cut down on travel time between the points by taking a shortcut, which invariably means going outdoors. But if you value the barrier between you and nature that the hotel provides, you might just opt for the longer route and choose to stay within the confines of the glass-walled corridor along with everyone else.

One modern alternative to the problems of horizontal extension is the Nevele's cylindrical guest-room "tower"; lower than its name implies, it does away with long corridors by arranging its rooms in a circle. The Brickman's grouping of rooms around courtyardlike spaces, and its ranch-house addition, are other measures for combating sprawl, and Mohonk's serendipitous off-set additions provide still another alternative to the long, bleak view down endless corridors.

When all building parts are linked, resort proprietors can claim that all rooms are in the "main building"—the social heart—no matter how far they may be from the actual geographical center. Thus the planning of these modern complexes has returned in effect to the grand-hotel scheme of the turn of the century, when new hotels were built to accommodate two or three hundred guests in a single great building, with everyone housed and entertained under one roof.

Public Spaces

Resort architecture has to accommodate changing tastes by providing specialized settings. The latest thing in resort entertainment in the 1880s was a formal dance in the ballroom; today it would be a famous television comedian or singer performing in the nightclub. The Mountain House had a ballroom on the second floor measuring 40 × 65 feet with a 12-foot ceiling. It was added to the hotel before 1844. In the 1890s, this seemed a cramped

This "Four Star" Vacation Spot of the Catskills Offers a New Theatre

The Nemerson Playhouse

NEMERSON guests will this year enjoy the elaborate theatre that has just been completed. The only two-story, steel structure of its kind in the Catskills, embodying a main floor with seating capacity of 800 and equal to the most exclusive Broadway Playhouse. The upper floor, with its Grand Ballroom and Lounge Rooms, has the modern decorations, comforts and conveniences of a new metropolitan hotel.

Vacation Guide, 1937, New York, Ontario & Western Railway, Barbara Purcell Collection

room; guests at fashionable hotels wanted something more soaring and glamorous for their balls. Today there is not a single Catskill resort that still provides a special ballroom; in a fairly typical move, Tennanah Lakeshore Lodge has turned its dance floor into an indoor pool.

Theatrical performance has always been a part of the Catskill resort experience. Lexington House, a former hotel which is now home to a theater company, provided performance space for local players beginning in the 1880s. Traveling opera, melodrama, and vaudeville troupes toured the area during the nineteenth century, performing at village theaters or in social halls frequented by hotel guests. Some hotels had their own theaters: in 1892, Churchill Hall in Stamford advertised a music hall with gas footlights. The 1920s saw an increased use of the mountains as a live performance center when talking pictures put many vaudeville entertainers out of work. The hotels came up with stages and halls for the audience, even when it meant moving dining tables out of the way, and it was then that the casino became a standard resort feature. This was a separate building with stage, lights, scenery, dance floor, movable seats, and perhaps a bar. Audiences were made up of hotel guests plus anyone else who would pay to get in. For many resorts today, the twenties or thirties casino building remains the entertainment center.

The 1950s saw a shift from the live, local-talent performances of the prewar era to acts by Broadway stars and then television stars—particularly in the newly prosperous Jewish resorts. Kids who had started their entertainment careers on Catskill stages and had gone on to make it in Hollywood came back and performed in the new nightclubs. The idea of a permanent nightclub was associated with drinking as well as entertainment, and the two were not compatible for the largely Jewish clientele until the postwar era. The Concord was first with a proper nightclub, followed by Kutsher's in 1954 and Brown's in 1957. Today the Concord's nightclub is the largest in the world, holding over

Hotel décor ranged from simple and rustic to grandiose, as in this nineteenth-century photograph of the parlor at Overlook Mountain House in Woodstock, opened in 1871. Evers Collection

three thousand guests. Kutsher's 1973 version seats up to two thousand. These large, single-purpose rooms have terraced floors leading down to the stage and a small dance floor just in front of the onstage band. Décor may be traditional, as at Brown's, with chandeliers and pilasters, or sleekly modern, as at Kutsher's or the Brickman. Color and lighting build in a permanent, sophisticated atmosphere.

Lobbies serve the resort hotel in two ways. As the first space the guest enters, the lobby gives initial direction to the stranger and sets the tone or style of the place. Thus when you enter Scott's at Oquaga Lake, furniture from years gone by, calico, woody colors, and intimate living-room scale welcome you to the family atmosphere, a little old-fashioned and very unpretentious. Off this central lobby, halls and stairs lead to the dining room, the guest rooms, television room (with a disapproving jingle about its users over the door), and the Scotts' private quarters.

At Kutsher's Country Club the lobby is vast and carpeted, with the registration desk at one end and islands of modular upholstered seating marking off areas to the other side. Modern, plush, yet quiet, the lobby projects a tone of contemporary tastefulness. Brown's lobby is also large, but it is focused on a fireplace—a domestic motif—rendered at hotel-lobby scale. The copper-hooded fireplace and the brown and orange tones of carpets and furnishings combine with chandeliers to set a tone of opulent/rustic/domestic, just right for the hotel's ambience. The Nevele's lobby, with its unashamedly fifties free-form terrazzo fountain, is the least domestic lobby in its associations, and conversely the most used for conversational gatherings, especially after dinner.

The dining room is the place where one finally gets a sense of how many guests there actually are in a given hotel: they assemble there at the same time, or within the same bracketed dinner hours, and tend to resemble an overwhelming sea, since the room is likely not to be broken down by any visual devices that might moderate its immense square footage. (An exception is the Concord, which serves two thousand guests in three dining rooms.) This is the only area in the hotel where such an enormous space is genuinely practical for the service performed; guests can size each other up, find out who's who, and socialize, all under the guise of eating a meal.

The architectural design of Catskill resort dining rooms tends to be minimal — more a matter of unimpeded progress from kitchen to always-hungry guest than the creation of real atmosphere. Early dining rooms were plainly furnished, with polished (and slippery) wooden floors, easy-to-move-chairs, and usually lots of windows. Since kitchen fires were often responsible for disasters, it was not untypical for a house to expand by erecting a separate building for its dining and kitchen facilities and turning over the original building to guest rooms and parlor functions. Every time a hotel expanded its guest-room capacity, it had to expand its dining facilities correspondingly, and many dining rooms, such as those at Grossinger's and the Sugar Maples, show successive stages of enlargement upon an original room.

Flexible, multi-use public spaces, both outdoors and in, are becoming less and less popular for modern Catskill resorts. Lawns which once doubled for playing tennis, croquet, badminton, or even baseball, have lost those functions, and today each sport has its own specialized courts and fields. The lawn's only contemporary function is to be lawnlike, setting off the resort buildings and looking plush and green. Frequent "keep off" signs help to ensure its inviolability. Likewise, interior spaces that once were convertible from dining hall to casino or theater are also purified of more than one function.

Early resort hotels made spaces flexible by means of folding doors. At the Catskill Mountain House, the folding doors extended down one side of the parlor "in some wild architectural dance," according to a contemporary observer, who concluded, "It is a dangerous room for a nervous man." Today at Scott's, the casino theater is used for movies, then chairs are moved away for dancing on the polished floor, and later a nightclub show is presented from the stage in the same room. Gavin's

Mohonk maintains an old-fashioned style in bedrooms where open windows invite breezes and capture views. Mohonk Mountain House, New Paltz, New York

nightclub serves equally well for Irish music and dancing at night and mass in the morning. But the modern trend is that the more flexible the space, the less fashionable it is; modern nightclub spaces are never used except for evening shows, as the built-in seating and the built-in atmosphere preclude the possibility of alternate usage.

The hotel is unusual among architectural types as a public building containing private facilities. The boundaries between these realms and the meanings and associations of *public* and *private* have changed substantially over the period of Catskill resort experience. The bedroom today is the only guaranteed area of privacy within the social world of most contemporary resorts. It is there that one finds rest and renewal for the entertainment and activity that fill most of resort time. It was not always so, however. Where we might retire to our rooms for a refreshing pause, our predecessors in the resorts would retire to nature, a practice so rare to resort-goers today that it distinguishes them as almost antisocial.

In the early inns and at lower-income places, guests shared rooms simply because there were not enough to go around. In the tradition of old English inns, sleeping was done dormitory style, and when the bedroom was crowded with roommates, the outdoors provided the privacy, relaxation, and refreshment to the spirit that were the point of going on vacation. In the twentieth century, when more luxurious hotels were able to offer private rooms, camp-style resorts still expected groups of strangers to share sex-segregated cottages, like the one called "Monastery" at the Sugar Maples.

When private rooms were available during the nineteenth century, bedroom sizes were small, although few records of actual dimensions have survived. In his book on the Catskill Mountain House, Roland Van Zandt notes that bedrooms there ranged from 7 × 10 feet to 15 × 15 feet. "The dormitory style of the earliest house of 1824 left a structural imprint upon later additions, creating an aspect of cellular uniformity throughout the sleeping quarters of the finished hotel." At the Kaaterskill, a luxury hotel built in 1881, every room was 16 feet deep from entrance door to window wall, and 9 to 12 feet wide.

Private bedroom comforts were minimal in the

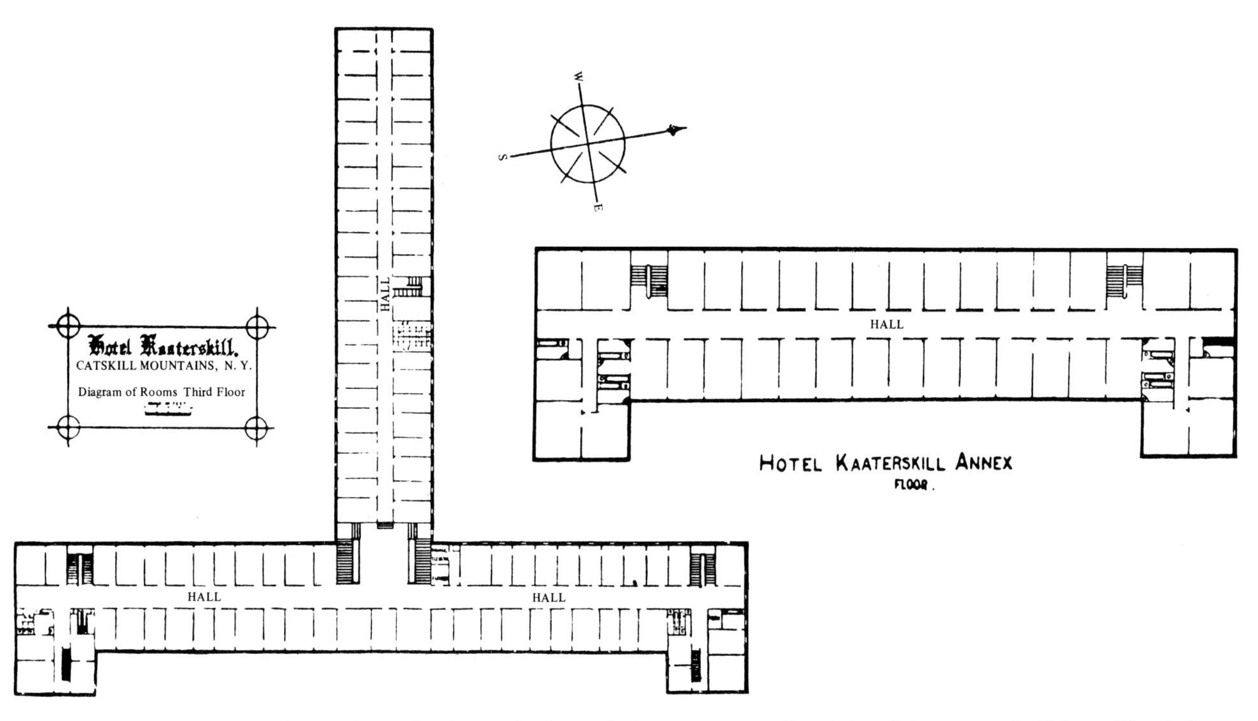

The Hotel Kaaterskill may have been a luxury hotel in its day, but its bedrooms were small and shared "an aspect of cellular uniformity" with the rival Catskill Mountain House. Hotel Kaaterskill brochure, undated, Evers Collection

early years. A pitcher of water and a basin for washing would be provided, but, except in the most expensive places, closets were unheard of. Until fairly recently, private bathrooms or toilets were available only for premium prices. Guests today who demand a sunken tub with whirlpool could have demanded no more than indoor plumbing as their luxurious due a century ago. In 1884, at the new and elegant Kaaterskill there were four hundred rooms, only fifty of which had private baths. Through the 1930s, hotels advertised bathtubs and showerbaths as special attractions, and many thriving resorts still have communal hall bathrooms in their older wings.

Today's newly constructed resort bedrooms are far more lavish than those in most private houses or apartments. Their walls are more soundproof, their ceilings higher, and their general dimensions more generous. Standard features of the contemporary Catskill resort bedroom include color television, wall-to-wall carpet, and a pair of queen-size beds. Modern times require a private bathroom for every bedroom, and bathrooms offer an entire new field for luxury: separate dressing room, extra sinks, sunken tub, and refrigerator. These quarters are so well equipped that one could almost live there permanently. The scale of comforts has increased handsomely since World War II; facilities that would have been considered generous for six are now normal for two, imparting a sense of the sybaritic to the ordinary private functions of the vacationer.

Style

If the identification of architectural styles in the Catskills is confused by the additive nature of the building process there, it is confused still further by the hotels' own original stylistic intentions. Advertisements of all periods show that hotels were most concerned with assuring their guests of solid comfort rather than fashionable architectural style. Thus the Tremper House was "furnished in hardwood, with marble top bureaux and tables; bedding of best South American hair, and Brussels carpets." Even when we do find a contemporaneous style description, it is often less than helpful. The Grand Hotel, 650 feet long, was described as "of the Queen Anne style, with projecting towers, giving to the building a cozy, homelike yet imposing effect."

While resort buildings have assumed all kinds of forms and all kinds of style variations and combinations, there were still moments in Catskill history when a certain type predominated at the more up-to-date places. (It should be noted that "up-to-date" is not a quality judgment but merely an indication that the management has paid special attention to current trends.)

In the later railroad era of the nineteenth century, the type that predominated was the wooden hotel structure, three to four stories high, planned as a long bar with perpendicular wings and identified by its long verandah. Found all along the eastern seaboard and throughout the Catskills at the turn of the century, these hotels were usually ornamented with jigsaw work, in a stylistic com-

Stucco as a fireproof material was successful metaphorically rather than literally, as shown by news photos of the fire at the old Savoy in Kiamesha Lake. There, visible under the coat of peeling stucco, is the wood, as flammable as it always had been. Manville Wakefield Collection; photo: Charlie Crist, 1967

posite of Italianate, Queen Anne, Second Empire, and whatever else came to hand. Most larger examples of this type no longer exist in the Catskills, having been lost more to fire than to modernization.

Stylistic consistency is found again in the stucco hotel of the 1920s and 1930s, especially in the southern Catskills. This style can be characterized as a closed, blockish building coated with stucco, three to four stories high, with a capacity of over one hundred guests. One reason for its popularity was that it appeared to be fireproof. The material *looked* like something that would not burn, and indeed it was a protective layer against fire. But the stucco was usually applied over the highly flammable wood construction that was then typical of almost all Catskill hotels. Stucco as a fireproof material was successful metaphorically rather than literally, as news photos of the fire at the old Savoy show: there, visible underneath the coat of peeling stucco, is the wood, as flammable as it always had been.

Stucco textures and detailing vary from the half-timbered look to the more decorative attempts at freehand swirls. One hotel owner asserts that you can tell the very year the stucco was applied to a Catskill hotel: in 1920 it was gray with a brushed-on texture; in 1925 it was white stucco with black and white pebbles pressed onto it, or yellow stucco with trowel marks for texture; in 1930 it was smooth stucco with wooden one-by-fives applied to make it "Tudor," Grossinger's trademark surface. Because Sullivan County experienced such a period of growth during the twenties and thirties, it is there that most examples of the stucco idiom are to be found.

The prevalence of stucco as a twenties favorite in Sullivan County makes many of its hotels look remarkably similar. The standard treatment of the verandah in that era, bounded by a flat parapet solidly filled in, is still another tendency toward suppressing their individuality. These hotels are frequently composed of three-story blocks, with the fourth floor consisting of dormers and towers: the Nemerson at South Fallsburg is an example. In the Stevensville of this period, a fifth floor is present, composed of octagonal tower rooms and a square central turret. Reminders of the turret motif remain today at Brown's, from its earlier years as the Black Appel Inn.

Another favorite motif of the stucco era is the fan window. On many ground floors, the large fan window in series opens up the interior to the sun and may even supplant the verandah as an "outdoorsy" place to sit. These expanses of many-paned glass give character to the otherwise rather bland stucco exterior, as seen at the Ratner (later Raleigh) or at the New Empire on White Lake. A comprehensive example is the early Concord building, in which fan windows stretched all the way across the façade. The quality of light in the interior of these rooms is especially appealing: in the Flagler sunroom, kinship with the outdoors is appealingly emphasized by the inclusion of indoor wicker furniture and many plants.

Because the ethnic character of many Catskill resorts is so striking, one might expect to find an "ethnic style" in their architecture too. But there is almost nothing in the architectural style of the resorts that connects to ethnic traditions in social life. The rare exception, the Bavarian Manor in Purling, with its Bavarian chalet and Tyrolean painted decorations, illuminates the situation. German décor and accouterments carry on the nineteenth-century tradition of the German beer garden and its band music, but the resort stands out as picturesque, not truly ethnic, and the clientele is entirely mixed and "American." Rather like going to Colonial Williamsburg, one goes to Bavarian Manor for atmosphere, not for genuine ethnic values.

For most groups in the Catskills, resort development did not immediately follow on the heels of immigration; it had to wait until immigrants could store up some savings, obtain jobs which provided a vacation, and feel comfortable enough in their new urban surroundings to risk leaving for still another unfamiliar place. Although the ethnic homogeneity of a Catskill resort is usually a comforting reminder of origins and home ties, the guests do not look to architectural style to reinforce their cultural traditions.

Corollary to the mobility among ethnic-group members, hotels themselves have a history of changing their ethnic orientations with a bill of sale. Subsequent changes in the buildings are directed toward enhanced comfort and modernity, not toward the switch in ethnic identity. Sunset Park Hotel in Haines Falls began as the focus for a private club community at the turn of the century, but it has catered to a Greek clientele since about 1940. Its Queen Anne style has not been altered at all; instead, a Greek band plays ethnic songs in the nightclub. The rule of architecture as a nonclue to ethnic identity is consistent throughout the Catskill resorts.

In the nineteenth century, A. J. Downing proposed that certain styles were sympathetic to certain kinds of scenery: the natural setting was supposed to welcome rustic, Tyrolean, or gothicizing modes, while the classical belonged in a setting of greater control and imposed order. Since the railroad era, Catskill resorts have largely followed this sense of matching. For this reason, the return to classicism of the 1890s, as seen in Chicago's White City or in the Newport palaces and their Fifth Avenue counterparts, does not seem to have had a noticeable influence on the Catskills. Even in hotels specifically built or expanded during the turn-of-the-century classical revival, taste tended toward some version of the picturesque, mansarded, castellated, towered, or "a veritable Swiss chalet," consummated in James Ware's work at Mohonk. A taste for the symmetry which is allied to classicism did show itself during the 1920s, but this was achieved without columns, pediments, or any pretentiousness.

There was also little attention paid to the Colonial revival, which has elsewhere been a pervasive twentieth-century idiom. Gas stations and supermarkets may have picked it up, but the Catskill resort hotels steadfastly preferred rustic referents — even down to the very modern resorts like Kutsher's Country Club, where stone textures complement the plate glass and earthy colors make a gesture toward the natural setting.

It is historically typical of Catskill styles that they never get too far from home. Styles and surfaces tend to stay within those acceptable for American domestic use—even if they are a bit exaggerated in such cases as the log-cabin–Scandinavian Mt. Pleasant Lodge or the half-timbered Friar Tuck. The resorts of California or Florida may please their customers with the amazing fantasies of the Madonna Inn or the Hollywood glamour of the Eden Roc, but the Catskill visitor seems to prefer the comfortable over the exotic.

Catskill architectural style has no single direction today. For the biggest resorts of Sullivan and Ulster counties, the trend is toward expanses of glass and concrete-and-steel construction. This usually results in a modernist aesthetic, but one with more texture and color than its urban counterpart. Modern materials for surfaces are preferred at all economic and taste levels; Formica, Fiberglas, and other surfaces that take wear and are easy to clean are always preferable under hotel conditions, as well as more likely to satisfy modern fire and building-code restrictions.

Architects are only infrequently responsible for

Munsels *History of Delaware County,* New York, 1880

the creation of Catskill resort buildings. For the most part, hotels are the product of collaboration between owner and builder, and often enough the owner is his own builder. Early mountain dwellers were resourceful folk who practiced several "professions." Mert Whitcomb's grandfather had a sawmill and lumber business; besides running his Winter Clove Hotel at Round Top, he sawed the wood for the construction of its additions. Mert himself is a farmer, woodsman, and maple-sugarer, and he also runs Winter Clove and builds its additions. We have already described how members of the Thompson family did their own building at Thompson House; they continue to design, construct, and decorate the interior of their new additions.

In Fleischmanns and a few other towns, there have been periods when so much resort building was going on at once that a town could support several builders. Melvin Mayes, a long-time resident of Fleischmanns, remembers when he was on building crews during the teens and the twenties with his father and his grandfather; they had so much practice in hotel building that they eventually erected buildings of their own design.

Sometimes an affluent or a more demanding owner hired an architect. In the case of the Kaaterskill, George Harding of Philadelphia determined to make a hotel to outshine the old Catskill Mountain House. He hired S. D. Button, the architect of a Cape May resort hotel, to design his new venture. The Kaaterskill became one of the few resorts to claim architectural significance; the furniture in 1884 was in the "newest Eastlake designs and of the richest descriptions," and the hotel's comfort and luxury were compared to those "in the heart of New York or Paris." From the 1880s into the early 1900s, the Smileys at Mohonk also used architects—Napoleon LeBrun and Sons, and James Ware—at different times, to add to their existing, anonymously designed hotel complex.

In recent years the approach has changed. While diverse in both visual and managerial style, the large Ulster and Sullivan County hotels share a single architect. Dennis Jurow, whose practice is in Middletown, New York, near his major clients, has been the architect for nearly every Borscht Belt palace for the last fifteen years. Now in his early forties, Jurow was trained at Pratt in Brooklyn, but he developed a fondness for the mountains while putting himself through school as a summer waiter. With the sense of the hotel industry he absorbed during those seasons, Jurow joined an established local hotel architect, Sid Schlieman. He expected some years of apprenticeship and, with any luck, a gradual rise to success. Instead, his boss retired unexpectedly a year after Jurow joined the firm, leaving the design of Sullivan County hotels in Jurow's astonished care. Now experienced in the hotel industry's needs and problems, Dennis Jurow is highly praised by all hotel owners for his ability to give them what they want. Jurow himself is very sensitive to each owner's needs for individuality of style, and he tries to make designs that enhance the hotel's—rather than the architect's—image.

The preceding pages have identified certain modern trends: the tendency to enclose circulation and porch spaces that once were open to nature; to build spaces that are specialized for a single use; to continually enlarge the facilities; and to join all separate buildings into one complex. But it is important to remember that only some of the Catskill resorts have elected modernity as their preferred style. Dozens of thriving resorts retain styles of the past, and original structures preserve the spirit of earlier resort experience. Challenging issues of preservation and reuse, along with a concern for the loss of our material past, are today reviving the strong appeal of buildings of an earlier period. The astonishing range of choice provided by the Catskill resorts—from the authentic old inn to the glistening country club — may prove to be one of the region's greatest strengths.

—*Elizabeth Cromley*

ELIZABETH CROMLEY, an architectural historian, teaches art history and architectural history at the City College of the City University of New York, where she is completing her doctoral dissertation on the development of the American apartment building in the nineteenth century.

CATSKILL PORTFOLIO

Photographs by John Margolies

The Catskill Mountains

THE INN

Windham House, Windham, New York.
Farmhouse built in 1800, porch added in 1869.

THE FARMHOUSE

Sugar Maples, Maplecrest, New York, 1915–present.
Resort takes over Main Street.

Thompson House, Windham, New York.
Spruce Cottage, 1893 (left); gazebo and Manor House porch, c. 1880.

The Hestoria, Durham, New York, date unknown.
Barn into boarding house.

Menges' Lakeside, Livingston Manor, New York, 1900 to present.
A farmhouse engulfed.

BUNGALOWS AND MOTELS

Marteen's Cabins, Marlboro, New York, c. 1925.

Osborn House, Windham, New York, c. 1930.
Separate bedrooms.

Villa Roma, Callicoon, New York.
A separate room for everyone.

Thompson House, Windham, New York.
Motel unit, 1962, with 1866 tower beyond.

THE SMALL HOTEL

Winter Clove, Round Top, New York.
Opened in 1836 and expanded over the years.

Tennanah Lakeshore Lodge, Roscoe, New York, c. 1930.
Sullivan County pagoda II.

Edgewood Inn, Livingston Manor, New York, c. 1925.
Twin-turreted two-tone.

Tempel Inn, Livingston Manor, New York, c. 1930.
Sullivan County pagoda I.

Bavarian Manor, Purling, New York.
Two-story, 1863 porch with balconies.

Hanson's Hotel, Deposit, New York.
Lake instead of lawn.

Polonia House, South Fallsburg, New York, c. 1930.
Closed 1976. Sullivan County stucco style.

THE LARGE HOTEL

Mohonk Mountain House, New Paltz, New York, 1870–1903.
One-eighth mile of additions.

Mohonk Mountain House, New Paltz, New York.
The lake's corner straddled.

Mohonk Mountain House, New Paltz, New York.
Thirty acres of landscaping.

Cliff House, Lake Minnewaska, New York, 1879.
Closed, 1972. Destroyed by fire, 1978.

Cliff House, Lake Minnewaska, New York.
White clapboard "stick style."

Cliff House porch, Lake Minnewaska, New York.

Cliff House entrance porch, Lake Minnewaska, New York.

Cliff House ruins, Lake Minnewaska, New York, 1978.

Granit Hotel, Kerhonkson, New York, c. 1970.
Rural high-rise.

Grossinger's, Grossinger, New York.
Sullivan County Tudor.

Concord Hotel, Kiamesha Lake, New York, 1920's–present.
The city in the country.

Concord Hotel, Kiamesha Lake, New York, 1978.
New wing.

THE VERANDAH

Winter Clove, Round Top, New York.

The Nevele Hotel and Country Club, Ellenville, New York, c. 1970.
Private porches.

Mohonk Mountain House, New Paltz, New York, 1900.

Fleischmanns Park Hotel gazebo, Fleischmanns, New York, c. 1890.

Campbell Inn, Roscoe, New York.
Porch frames view.

THE CORRIDOR

Grossinger's, Grossinger, New York, c. 1960.
"Verandah" into parlor.

Mohonk Mountain House, New Paltz, New York, c. 1890.
Corridor as parlor.

Hotel Brickman, South Fallsburg, New York, c. 1965.
Just like outdoors.

Raleigh Hotel, South Fallsburg, New York, c. 1970.
Stairways everywhere.

Mohonk Mountain House, New Paltz, New York.

Kutsher's Country Club, Monticello, New York, c. 1970.
Corridor links the pieces.

THE LOBBY AND THE PARLOR

Hanson's Hotel wicker parlor, Deposit, New York, date unknown. Closed, 1977.

Scott's Oquaga Lake House, Deposit, New York, c. 1920.
An old-fashioned lobby.

The Nevele Hotel lobby, Ellenville, New York, c. 1955.
Miles of carpet and free-form fountain.

Mohonk Mountain House main parlor, New Paltz, New York, 1900.
Two-story rustic splendor.

Mohonk Mountain House parlor exterior, New Paltz, New York.
"A veritable Swiss chalet."

THE DINING ROOM

Mohonk Mountain House dining room, New Paltz, New York, 1891–92.
Meal with a view.

Concord Hotel dining room, Kiamesha Lake, New York, 1946.
Two thousand guests per sitting.

THE NIGHTCLUB

Scott's Oquaga Lake House casino, Deposit, New York, c. 1920.

Woodlawn Showboat, White Lake, New York, c. 1925.

Emerald Isle Hotel Tavern, South Cairo, New York, date unknown.
Resort's neighborhood bar.

Kutsher's Country Club, Monticello, New York, 1973.
Blue romance.

THE BEDROOM

Concord Hotel bedroom, Kiamesha Lake, New York, 1978.
The newest and the plushest.

ATHLETIC FACILITIES

Brown's Hotel pool, Loch Sheldrake, New York, c. 1965.

Old hotel pool, South Fallsburg, New York, date unknown.

Scott's Oquaga Lake House boathouse, Deposit, New York, c. 1880.

Menges' Lakeside boathouse, Livingston Manor, New York.

Handball backboards.

Rose's Cottages, Monticello, New York.

Brentwood Cottages, Loch Sheldrake, New York.

Lorraine Hotel, Lake Huntington, New York.

THE GUESTS

Group from Lorain, Ohio. Scott's Oquaga Lake House, Deposit, New York.

Grossinger's, Grossinger, New York.
Poolside.

Hotel Mathes entrance, Fleischmanns, New York.

Awosting Falls, Lake Minnewaska, New York.

JOHN MARGOLIES, photographer and critic, has exhibited his work at the Cooper-Hewitt Museum and the Museum of Modern Art, New York. He lectures widely on the culture of American vernacular design and has produced several video pieces, among which is a study of Catskill resorts.

Going to the Mountains: A Social History

It is the guests as much as the architecture who have created the distinctive resort landscape of New York's Catskill Mountains. From the road, the resort buildings reveal little about the identity of these guests. Only as the visitor moves closer and watches Italians playing boccie at Villa Maria, hears the strains of a Protestant hymn from the Mohonk parlor, eats a Sunday brunch at Grossinger's, or listens to Armenian music, Irish witticisms, Yiddish punchlines, or Yankee understatements do the identities become tangible. The food, the family patterns, the games, the languages and dress, the humor — these are the qualities that create distinctive resort atmospheres. And the Catskill resorts are as diverse as the cities they serve.

The social history of the Catskills as a resort landscape is closely linked to the history of eastern industrial cities, especially New York. The proximity of the mountains allowed early and easy access, which translated into relatively low travel costs. From the mid-nineteenth century, the Catskills began to develop resort forms which extended the luxury of the summer vacation to the broadening urban middle class. Since the beginning of the twentieth century, the history of the resorts has reflected not only the gradual popularization of the vacation experience, but the upward mobility of New York's ethnic groups — especially its Jewish population. In the last twenty-five years, the extension of leisure time and the improved standard of living of increasing numbers of city dwellers have extended the reach, as well as the comforts, of the Catskill resorts.

Resorts are distinctive environments in that they serve private living habits in a public sphere. Living among strangers for a week or for a summer, guests have always needed some minimal reassurance that they would find mutual respect and understanding. That guarantee is the essence of the "homeyness" of Catskill hotels. The social life of the resorts has reflected the personal and group values of their guests, whether those values are expressed in dietary laws, religious observances, manners, or styles of entertainment. As in the cities, Catskill guests have sought out company of a common social and ethnic background and of a common economic condition. The very multiplicity and variety of people "going to the mountains" over the last century has created the paradox of clusterings and exclusions within individual hotels. Far from simply Americanizing immigrant guests, the resorts have often affirmed ethnic values and community. The Catskill resort landscape remains peculiarly insular — today, almost suburban — reflecting less an urge to "get away from it all" than the impulse to transport the sociability, the conveniences, and the amusements of the city to the mountains.

The categories used to describe different kinds of Catskill resorts are sometimes ambiguous, for they depend on social organization as much as on physical plant. Bungalows, camps, boarding houses, hotels, or kocheleins ("cook-alones") often refer less to the shape of the buildings than they do to the arrangement of meals. In kocheleins and bungalow colonies, guests bring their own food and linen, and serve, cook, and entertain themselves. At boarding houses, hotels, and adult camps, the resorts provide the meals. Yet sometimes resorts with bungalows—or indeed, hotels with tents—include central dining halls, and buildings which house kocheleins may look like private Catskill farmhouses from the outside. One hotel, embracing the identity crises inherent in the labels, called itself a "country club farm inn."

IN THE WOODS

Thomas Nast, *Harper's Weekly*, July 21, 1866,
The Bronck Museum Collection

For guests, the distinction among types was usually as clear as whether the family had to wash dishes after dinner. The decision about which type of resort to go to turned, of course, on economics. Though some might prefer a family vacation that includes cooking and cleaning for themselves, many of those who grew up with Catskill summers remember the family move from cook-your-own to hotels as a significant step up the social ladder. Because "hotels" imply more complete service, a larger number of guests, and often the presence of liquor, they have also assumed the subjective connotations of higher status. Yet hotels themselves have sought to retain the more intimate and personally hospitable connotations of the "house," "inn," and especially the "summer home." For those families who return every year to the same place, many resorts succeeded in merging the luxury of a vacation with the intimacy of home.

As the buildings have adapted and changed over the years, so, too, has the organization of resort life in the Catskills. Contradictions to the surviving ethnic styles make simple stereotyping impossible —roast beef for dinner at an Italian resort, black guests at a hotel which fifty years ago advertised its all-white kitchen staff, increasing as well as decreasing orthodoxy at different Jewish hotels. The resorts which once featured their country virtues have now embraced suburban ease. Many have gone from being "summer homes" to becoming weekend retreats. Large hotels have discovered that their guests increasingly want greater privacy in their hotel living arrangements, even as they expect more organized social programs and new packaged diversions. Yet those guests who return summer after summer also carry with them familiar and personal traditions, friends, and habits that preserve the sense of continuity which has been so large a part of Catskill resort life. The changes are sufficiently gradual that guests have always known what to expect in the Catskills. For one hundred fifty years, they have expected their own good company, a homey atmosphere, special entertainments, convenience, and more food than they can comfortably eat.

Rip Van Winkle Climbed Here

Today the word *Catskills* triggers two associations: the mountains themselves and the resorts. The two are inseparable, and, to many guests, indistinguishable. The resorts are there because of the mountains—or vice versa; sometimes it is hard to remember which came first. Guests at hotels today do not often discuss the scenery. They feel comfortable with the view, and they enjoy it as a recurring reminder that they have left the city behind. Yet often their contact with the mountains is mediated and framed by the window of a car, of a dining room, or of an indoor pool. In the nineteenth century, the first guests at Catskill resorts traveled to the mountains expressly to view and marvel at the scenery. The Catskills were the mountains.

Nature was the first attraction of the Catskill resorts. "A few years ago this delightful retreat was almost unknown," an 1834 travel guide reported. "At length the tale of the extent and beauty of the prospect and the grandeur of the scenery drew attention of individuals of taste; and the glowing descriptions they gave . . . effectively roused and fixed the attention of the public." "Individuals of taste" included such storytellers as James Fenimore Cooper and Washington Irving, and artists such as Thomas Cole, Asher Durand, and Benjamin Stone. When the Catskill Mountain Association opened the Pine Orchard House (later the Mountain House) in 1823, as the Catskills' first resort hotel, well-to-do Americans and Europeans began stopping there on the rigorous Grand Tour from Niagara Falls to Boston. With sensibilities already predisposed to find the sublime in nature, travelers carried their palettes, sketchbooks, and diaries with them to capture and record the effect of the mountains. They also joined in the already popular mountain sports of fishing and hunting as another way of establishing contact with nature.

Painters and writers of the Romantic school at the beginning of the nineteenth century left later Catskill visitors the legacy of their enthusiasm and reverence for the power and harmony of nature. They looked to the stirring and uplifting — even

THE KAATERSKILL FALLS.

"When we first saw the falls in the full 'joy of light and sound,' leaping, exulting, careering over the dark ragged rocks, into the amphitheater overhung with precipices and forest, the sight was imposing in the extreme ... There is usually a person at the shanty above whose business it is to deal out the sublime by the shilling's worth by raising the sluice of the saw mill." *New York Mirror,* May 14, 1834. *Boarding House Directory,* 1887, Evers Collection

THE PHOTOGRAPHER.

Thomas Nast, *Harper's Weekly*, July 21, 1866, The Bronck Museum Collection

transcendent—prospects of the mountains to divert tired imaginations from the "irksome monotony of the world below." An inspiring view invited contemplation of the higher natural and spiritual order. These Romantics exercised a selective vision in viewing the landscape: they did not see or record the tanneries which covered the hemlock hillsides with pits and smokestacks, nor in later years the Catskill furniture factories and textile mills, or their workers.

In 1866, Charles Baldwin, a typical visitor, described in his diary a day trip and picnic at the Kaaterskill Falls:

> After looking at the fall from in front as long as we wished, Sarah, Lizzie, Mary Monmor, Peter Stewart and myself went across in front of the fall, and then along the path which leads around back . . . where we sat down to gaze upon the beautiful scenery before us. While we were here, the water-gates above the fall were opened and a tremendous volume of water poured down in front of us. . . . The concussion produced by this great mass of water plunging from a height of 180 feet to the pool below, fairly shook the dome of rock above and around us; and the roar of the waterfall echoed and re-echoed among the hills and valleys. All those with me sat speechless until the great flood of water ceased and the fall resumed its ordinary proportions; and then all mentioned it as one of the grandest sights they ever beheld.

The Kaaterskill Falls were the most awesome natural feature of the Catskills. Countless visitors, from the fictitious Leatherstocking to Justice Joseph Story, recorded their impressions of the falls. But as one skeptical guest observed, "if your romantic nerves can stand the truth, the Catskill Falls is turned on to accommodate poets and parties of pleasure." Indeed, the falls were worked by a gate which allowed their "manager" to dam the waters and then to turn them on when enough people had gathered and paid twenty-five cents for the effect. Discovering the drawing power of the natural landscape, Catskill resort proprietors learned early to manipulate nature to please their guests. Few visitors departed unimpressed by the unleashing of the Kaaterskill Falls, however channeled by local impresarios.

Hotels sited on cliffs overlooking the mountains and valleys maximized the exposure of their guests to the view. Landscaped paths and coaching roads led through the "wilderness" to scenic vistas. These roads, starting with the early turnpikes, in effect tamed the mountains and opened them to the genteel travelers who had the time and money to pursue the sublime. Those on the grand tour indulged in comparisons between the American wilderness and scenes in Switzerland and Norway.

Even during the romantic period of Catskill hotels, resort guests sought something more than unmediated nature. They wanted a nature they could enjoy selectively, and in style. One of the grand hotels of Greene County featured the triumphant reconciliation of nature and *haute* civilization: "The grounds of the hotel embrace many acres of spacious lawn and wooded Alpine cliffs; terraced walks surround the house and grounds which are laid out in pretty grass plots, interspersed with flowers and shrubbery, and in the centre a magnificent fountain . . . the views from the Grand Hotel are Alpine in character . . . unlike any other in the mountains." Another contemporary declared, "The Pine Orchard is the resort of so much company during the pleasant season of the year that the attractions of its scenery are redoubled by the presence of agreeable and refined society."

As access to the mountains eased with the advent of railroads, the natural landscape itself became less awesome and intimidating to guests. Day trips to the falls and picnics to resort hotels brought nature into familiar reach. Where the Romantics had found in the natural landscape the hand of Omnipotence, later visitors discovered sentimental resemblances to fanciful beasties. One dour observer complained of the degeneration of guests who were

> afflicted with that disordered imagination which delights in finding the distorted form of an elephant or crocodile, floating as a cloud in the sky, and sees all sorts of horrid menagerie beasts, birds, and reptiles . . . in rock and tree and mountain outline. . . . Tysterneyck [mountain] 'is so interesting, you know' because it is supposed to resemble a recumbent tiger who lies with his head between his forepaws—in wait, let us hope, for these same misguided people, to devour once and for all their peculiar mental affliction.

For the first fifty years of the life of Catskill resorts, getting there was half the fun. As one traveler noted in 1881, looking back on the "old days" two decades before, "People who came for recreation were jostled up into the mountains by the great lumbering coaches—an experience that no sane person ever was ambitious to incur twice for mere enjoyment's sake." A new road in the 1880s to the Hotel Kaaterskill, perched, like the Mountain House, on a cliff, had not seemed to improve matters, for the road "had been cut right out of the side of [the] mountain. It is about four miles long and goes past the many gullies and chasms of the mountain without a single bridge. In many places, if the wagon wheel should go a foot out of the beaten track, the vehicle and its occupants would be half a mile further down the mountain in very short order." The limited access of the magnificently sited hotels of Greene County threatened their very success as resorts. Looking at the Pine Orchard, one traveler concluded, "Its appearance is very much that of a small white cloud in the midst of heaven and is in the highest degree wild and romantic. But I came to the conclusion, after gazing at it a considerable time, that the fatigue of climbing to the summit would be infinitely greater than the pleasure which its airy situation could afford."

"People who came for recreation were jostled up into the mountains by great lumbering coaches—an experience that no sane person was ambitious to incur twice for mere enjoyment's sake." *New York Times,* July 4, 1881. Thomas Nast, *Harper's Weekly,* July 21, 1866, The Bronck Museum Collection

One key to the success of later Catskill resorts was the elimination of effort and fatigue—and of risk—in getting to them. The Ontario and Western Railroad, which came to Sullivan County in the 1870s, and the Ulster and Delaware Railroad, through Ulster, Greene, and Delaware counties, allowed travelers to reach their destinations in half a day — a considerable improvement on the day-and-a-half often spent going by steamboat and coach to the lofty piazza of the Mountain House. Once settled, tourists could choose mountain climbing as an activity rather than bear it as an essential part of their journey; they were free to appreciate nature by means other than direct confrontation.

"Only the Best of People . . ."

"For months you have been breathing a second-hand, warmed over air," the Ulster and Delaware Railroad announced to its customers in the 1880s. "Now you must pack your grip and flee to the distilleries of the skies!" Beginning in the late 1870s, the advent of regularly scheduled railroads launched a new era for American resorts. Steamboats and railroads established access to the mountains with reasonable rates and regular timetables, and then vigorously promoted the benefits of resort travel. In the second half of the nineteenth century, thousands of city dwellers in New York, eastern Pennsylania, and New Jersey welcomed the promise of mountain-distilled pure air and began taking vacations not simply to view the inspiring scenery, but to protect and restore

THE

CATSKILL MOUNTAIN RAILWAY,

FROM CATSKILL LANDING, ON THE HUDSON RIVER,

TO THE

CATSKILL MOUNTAINS,

IS THE

Shortest, Quickest and Best Route

TO THE

Catskill Mountain House and Hotel Kaaterskill, Haines' Falls, Tannersville, Laurel House, Palenville, Cairo, Durham, Windham, and Other Points in the Catskill Mountain Region.

Passengers for HOTEL KAATERSKILL and CATSKILL MOUNTAIN HOUSE can reach either Hotel

ONE TO TWO HOURS EARLIER BY THIS ROUTE

Than by any other.

Guests can BREAKFAST AFTER 8 A. M. at the above Hotels and reach New York *by this route* at 2.15 P. M.

Time, Expense and Over Fifty Miles of Travel Saved

By this route to Tourists from or to Saratoga.

Summer Boarders returning from Tannersville and vicinity should not fail to drive down the Mountains through the **FAMOUS KAATERSKILL CLOVE** and take passage by this road from Palenville to Catskill.

CLOSE CONNECTIONS MADE AT CATSKILL

With the Hudson River Day Line Steamers, and
The Steamers of the Catskill Night Line:
The N. Y. Central & Hudson River R. R., and
West Shore Railroad.

THREE TRAINS Each Way Daily in June. SIX DAILY TRAINS Each Way in July, August, September.

THROUGH TICKETS should be purchased as follows:

To LEEDS, for Leeds and vicinity.

To CAIRO, *via* the New **CAIRO RAILROAD** Extension, for CAIRO, FREEHOLD, EAST DURHAM, OAK HILL, DURHAM, ACRA, SOUTH DURHAM, EAST WINDHAM AND WINDHAM.

To LAWRENCEVILLE. for Lawrenceville and Kiskatom.

To MOUNTAIN HOUSE STATION, for Catskill Mountain House and Laurel House.

To PALENVILLE, for Palenville, Hotel Kaaterskill, Haines' Falls, Hilton House and Tannersville.

Carriages from the above Stations to the various Resorts.

The Railroad and Equipment are first-class in every respect,

and trains on this road make the time advertised.

THE ROAD WILL BE IN OPERATION DURING THE SEASON OF SUMMER TRAVEL.

CHAS. A. BEACH, Gen'l Sup't and Pass. Ag't,
CATSKILL, N. Y.

Boarding House Directory, 1887, Evers Collection

"Here upon the lofty border of this pure lake, among the wooded and rocky cliffs and heights, with rustic arbors and romantic walks, the company—only the best of people, quiet, intelligent, and well-to-do—love to dwell; always cool and comfortable without a bar or ball room." Mohonk brochure, 1893. Mohonk Mountain House, New Paltz, New York

their health as well.

Well-to-do Americans had begun going to resorts for their health even in the eighteenth century, escaping the summer cholera and yellow fever epidemics of the port cities. During the colonial period and the early nineteenth century, prosperous guests had assembled at Newport, Saratoga Springs, Ballston Spa, and Virginia Springs, to take the waters after the fashion of England's famed Bath. Later, seashore resorts also sprang up to cater to those guests who sought a change of scene and pace. By the mid-nineteenth century, steamboat travel had opened access to the Catskill region, Charles Beach had opened a regular summer season of balls and entertainments at the Mountain House, and conventional wisdom recommended taking the air as much as taking the waters.

The "sanitary awakening" movement in American cities following the Civil War heightened awareness of the environmental causes of disease and reinforced the popular association of the countryside with health. The steady growth of cities in the second half of the nineteenth century, and especially the new waves of immigration between 1890 and 1920, transformed urban living. By 1880, over two million people lived within a day's travel of the Catskills, and, by 1920, the New York-Philadelphia-New Jersey metropolitan region contained over eight million people.

Eastern industrial cities suffered from overcrowded living conditions, especially in the central immigrant ghettos, and from inadequate sanitation and the pollution of coal-fueled factories. To many genteel city dwellers, urban growth and change threatened not only public health and morals, but their control over their own private living environments. The more affluent began to move uptown or to new suburbs in a search for clean air and more space, and in a desire to escape the multitudes. In contrast to the menacing congestion of the industrial cities, the mountain resorts seemed to offer less the romantic wilderness of the past than the healthful, moral atmosphere of the country. Railroads, recognizing the increasing concern with ventilation and fresh air, and the attraction of uncontaminated country-fresh food, stressed these healthful properties as part of the promotion of their own resort hotels and other "summer homes" in the Catskills.

An emerging vacation ideology advocated escape from the city as preventive medicine as well as cure. Furthermore, a secularized view of nature recommended the mountain setting to give "overworked" businessmen, professionals, and clerks relief from the pressures of the urban pace. The rationale for summer vacations increasingly included the psychological as well as the physiological benefits of a change of scene and atmosphere.

MOUNTAIN VIEW FARM HOUSE.

(*P. O. Address, Catskill, N. Y.*) **FREDERICK SAXE, Proprietor.**

THIS PLEASANTLY SITUATED FARM HOUSE IS

Seven Miles from the Landing and One and a Half Miles from Catskill Mountain Railroad,

COMMANDING A

FINE VIEW OF MOUNTAINS AND MOUNTAIN HOUSE.

The surroundings on all sides are pleasant to the eye. Shady Groves near the house. Extensive Meadows, Trout Streams, &c. Table supplied with Vegetables, Butter, Milk and Eggs,

FRESH FROM THE FARM.

OUR OWN CONVEYANCE WILL MEET YOU—either at the Landing of the Day Boats, Catskill Night Boats, or at the Railroad Stations—by giving notice.

DAILY MAILS. ACCOMMODATION FOR FORTY GUESTS.

"Every farm house of any size is every summer converted into a rustic hotel. Though frequently crowded closely, these cozy homes are full of comfort." *New York Times*, July 4, 1881. *Boarding House Directory*, 1887, Evers Collection

The 1892 brochure of the Ulster and Delaware Railroad matter-of-factly summarized the attractions of Catskill resorts for the urban middle and upper classes:

> In the cities of the temperate zones, summer is the most enticing season in the country, and the most repulsive and unendurable in the city. Business is dull then, and there is little excuse for remaining in town. Your wife is sick and tired of society and town gayety, the children long for the annual romp amid the green hills and valleys. . . . The whole family is gasping for fresh air and the country. The demon Malaria threatens if you tarry, and the risk of delay is dangerous to assume. Thus it is, and wisely, that people dismiss their servants, lock up their town houses, pack up some necessary wearing apparel, and buy tickets for the mountains. Then, after a month or two of real country life, they return with renewed courage and vigor.

The grand hotels of the railroad era — the Kaaterskill, Mohonk, Overlook Mountain House — cultivated in the mountains a special setting for the enjoyment of leisure life. With extensive grounds featuring vast lawns, gardens, and landscaped walks leading to "spontaneous" vistas of spectacular scenery, these hotels invited a guest "to imagine that he is the owner of a great estate . . . [or] beside a lake in Switzerland." With a summer suspension of city responsibilities and identities, guests of these hotels could partake of the rituals of tea, croquet, lawn tennis, coaching parties, and cotillions. If the true elite could afford trips to Switzerland and private summer homes, the expanding middle class, supported by business and the professions, exercised its taste for propriety and decorum in a setting which nurtured family and religion. Arriving for six-to-ten-week stays with personal servants in tow, many of the guests perceived the summer resort as a natural extension of their winter homes and lifestyles. One guest found Mohonk "as near a perfect place as one can find away from his own home."

Many of the hotels of the 1880s and 1890s catered to the morale of their guests with a moral intensity. Mohonk was founded by Alfred and Albert Smiley, Quaker twin brothers who espoused a philosophy of resort management that featured just such a soothing, moral atmosphere, enhanced by "stimulating" company: "Here upon the lofty border of this pure lake, among the wooded and rocky cliffs and heights, with rustic arbors and romantic walks, the company — only the best of people, quiet, intelligent, refined and well-to-do — love to dwell; always cool and comfortable without a bar or a ballroom." Like the Smileys, Mohonk's upstanding clientele of professionals and clergy maintained a belief in the restorative value of vacations strong enough to absolve them of any guilt about their pursuit of leisure. Smiley even organized conferences on contemporary problems—

such as the "Indian question" — which allowed progressive guests to combine vacations with their interests in social reform.

Not everyone, however, went to the mountains for summer rest or moral enlightenment. While the guests of Mohonk heard sermons and nature talks, others at nearby Greene County hotels pursued the less uplifting diversions of a full social season. *The New York Times* society notes of the 1880s followed the guests and amusements of the Hotel Kaaterskill, Pine Hill, and of the private Twilight Park with the same avid attention given to the posh circles of Saratoga and the doings at the private summer homes of the very rich. In the public imagination, the Catskill resorts came to represent settings where "aesthetic furnishings, luxurious tables, seductive music, charming companions, well-graded drives, shaded walks, a bracing air, and a glorious view offer everything to be desired in the way of eating, drinking, dancing, flirting, making merry, and enjoying life to its utmost." The 1883 commentator added that "The Catskills offers its prodigal wealth to millionaires and those of limited means alike."

A SUMMER BOARDER'S LAMENT.

At morn I hear the fowls responsive,
While the milkman sings;
The mules' sad wail, the pigs' shrill squeal, and
Other dulcet things;
And when these truly rural beauties
Strike mine ear, my nose, mine eye,
'Tis then for thee, fair Babylon—
'Tis then for thee I sigh.

At noon, when o'er my smoking platter
I sit and sigh awhile,
And try the bread, which tastes like batter,
Spread with yellow "ile,"
And when the onions' tender breathings
Float in on the sultry air,
I wipe my streaming eyes and sigh
For Babylon the fair.

But when at night the tramps are prowling
And the night-hawks cry,
When sadly comes the farm dog's howling,
And the June bugs fly,
'Tis then I'd rise and shake the country
And the hay seed from my hair;
'Tis then to thee, fair Babylon,
Thy daughter would repair.

A Lone New-Yorker.

Harper's Bazaar, July 27, 1887

Contemplating the night view from the verandah of the Mountain House in 1881, one visitor remarked that "these other lights that twinkle all about like stars, only that we look down upon them instead of up, these are farmhouses and boarding houses." More than any other institution, boarding houses shaped the Catskill resort landscape by opening summer vacations to a new segment of the population — the modest middle class. Farmers had begun taking summer boarders to supplement their insufficient agricultural incomes even before the Civil War. In the railroad era at the turn of the century, both local and nonresident proprietors opened hundreds of boarding houses and farmhouses; they extended along the routes of the Ontario and Western Railroad through Sullivan County, and the Ulster and Delaware Railroad in the northern part of the Catskills. Some Catskill towns, such as Fleischmanns and Pine Hill, consisted almost entirely of hotels, boarding houses, farmhouses, and summer cottages. Between 1885 and 1915, farms and boarding houses dominated the resort scene with buildings which housed anywhere from ten to one hundred guests. With accommodations for ten thousand people altogether, these resorts constituted small cities of boarders.

Given the considerable differences between their incomes and working schedules and those of the wealthy guests of the large hotels, boarding-house and farmhouse guests adopted their own pattern of resort life. Those who were clerks, salaried managers, shopkeepers, or young professionals often came for two weeks at a time, paying the $6.00 to $12.00 per week which roughly equaled a week's salary. In contrast, the July-September Mohonk bill for Mr. and Mrs. Burnham—including the costs for their daughter and their maid, for a variety of day guests and visitors, and for two horses—came to just over $1,500.00, well over a year's salary for many farmhouse guests. Those boarding-house guests who stayed for the season — women who were the wives and mothers of the new urban white-collar class, and teachers and clergy who encouraged temperance—set a tone of churchgoing wholesomeness for many boarding houses at the turn of the century.

While the retreat to the mountains continued to offer as its greatest attraction fresh air and the relaxation of a vacation pace, it also promised "pleasurable excitement" to guests, who numbered seventy thousand a season in 1883, and four hundred thousand by 1906. Some observers grew skeptical of the social motives of resort-goers. Progressive reformer James Ford complained of the self-consciousness of status-driven people "who are absolutely insensible to the allurements of ocean or forest, but who nevertheless go somewhere out of town every summer of their lives — partly on the plea of health, or change of air and scene; partly in hope that the holiday journey will bring something new into their lives and extend their circle of acquaintances; but chiefly because everyone else who claims to be anybody at all makes a practice of going into the country during the hot weather." This is a refreshingly candid observation of the fact that resorts have long served as stages for the drama of social mobility.

Theater and masquerades, both on stage and off, have long amused Catskill guests. Newspaper "Summer Notes" reported one such "Original vaudeville sketch" at the Squirrel Inn in Twilight Park: "The Misses Pitken of Boston, the Misses Hill of New York and Miss Grant of Vassar enacted the roles of various squirrels, presenting a scene of forest gayety interspersed with topical songs in so unique a manner as to require frequent repetition." *New York Times*, August 5, 1906. *Boarding House Directory*, 1887, Evers Collection

Appropriately, a favorite resort theatrical event was the masquerade ball, held frequently during the Season. Every summer's social notes reported masked balls, some set around themes, others simply left to the random fantasy of guests who wished to playact. As many observers noted, the acting was not all play, and the masquerade continued beyond the scheduled nights. Guests arriving with their newly purchased summer wardrobes (which often consumed the better part of winter savings) might disguise their true material circumstance in order to attract other guests of a better "class," an exercise not confined to the nineteenth century.

In contrast to some of the large, more aloof hotels with their extensive and self-contained grounds, boarders at converted farmhouses and small hotels both participated in and helped create the community life of Catskill towns. Describing Pine Hill, one visitor noted that "where the entertainment of summer guests becomes an art involving the interests of an entire community as here, it should certainly reach perfection." At the turn of the century, townspeople and boarding-house guests alike shared in baseball, church fairs, county fairs, holiday celebrations, hayrides, and such special events as coaching day. When Liberty, a town with over eighty summer boarding houses and farmhouses, held its annual Coaching Day, wagons, buggies, and surreys came from hotels and boarding houses for miles around, each decorated with flowers and costumed guests illustrating an appropriate theme. Liberty's 1897 Coaching Day drew fifteen thousand people to see one hundred fifty decorated wagons. A float satirizing boarding-house life at "Coaching House" won the day's prize.

Dependent on the summer boarding population as a major source of income, in the years from 1890 to 1910, many towns sought to attract more boarders by undertaking village improvements, ranging from new roads to the installation of sewer systems and electricity. The resort communities of towns also drew strength from the constant exchanges and visits of guests among different boarding houses and hotels.

Boarding houses also paid the larger luxury hotels the compliment of imitation on a small scale. Like satellites, they clustered around these hotels, and their guests made numerous day trips and picnic excursions to view the grounds and manners of those who supported their genteel sensibilities with genteel incomes. Like the larger hotels, boarding houses offered the amusements of lawn sports such as croquet and tennis, and, when they could afford it, evening music and parlor dancing.

Where boarding houses were indeed the homes of their proprietors, the resort owners assumed the responsibility of the host for seeing that the guests were enjoying themselves. Yet even within the informal traditions and the light-handed direction of evening entertainment, hotels generally left the program during the day to the guests themselves. Some, like the locally renowned Misses Jordan of Haines Falls, filled the day unfailingly with a seven-mile walk "round the block" between each meal. Guests who admired the rural way of life assisted local farmers with haying and other chores. But for less driven souls, time could rest heavily when there were only so many postcards to be sent in a week.

Though most boarding houses had the essential facilities of the small resort — lawn sports, shuffleboard, bowling, and occasionally billiards and swimming (if they were situated near a natural watering hole) — many of the farms and houses offered only the view and the well-beaten walk to the town drugstore to amuse their more active guests. One former guest remembers the excruciating tedium of the unbroken day's sequence from the dining room to the verandah to the drugstore to the dining room to the post office to the verandah to the dining room to the verandah to bed.

In the end, eating good food took precedence over most other activity in the mountains. Hotels promoted the value of their farm-fresh milk and eggs "to prepare the delicate women and children for the hard city winter." And in 1905, the *Brooklyn Eagle* recommended mountain climbing as a sport "which brings every muscle into play and sends the blood coursing through the arteries at a faster rate,

Summer guests at the Soper Place (later Thompson House) in Windham, New York, c. 1885. John D. Goettsche Collection

creating a ravenous appetite and routing dyspepsia and insomnia." The central place of meals in the schedule assured the guests that, however bored they might become, there was compensation at dinner.

Though home and family are recurring motifs in the history of Catskill resorts, the large hotels did not always know quite what to do with the children. One hotel in 1903 advertised that its rooms were "large, airy, and arranged for the convenience of families," but, as though wary of the results of its own homey attractiveness, added "only a limited number of children taken." The Cragsmore struck a more harmonious chord by promising vaguely to provide children "freedom with safety." Part of that safety in the plush hotels came from supervision by nursemaids and governesses, for the children dined and slept with the servants. The young could eat with their parents, but it would cost more.

Most nineteenth-century guests at the grand hotels came either alone, as couples, or with friends; few took a "family vacation." But by the turn of the century the picture was changing. Boarding houses were a "children's paradise," according to the *Brooklyn Eagle* in 1905. And "the large hotels have playgrounds devoted exclusively to children, and in every region they will find cool brooks, and pebbly shores that are lined with shade trees." As an offspring of the progressive playground movements in the cities, such special children's facilities as playgrounds and a "children's parlor" began to appear at some resorts. More often, however, hotels and boarding houses still relied on the greater out-of-doors to amuse their young guests. Despite occasional advertisements noting "special care given to children," for the most part adults and children shared whatever entertainment the grounds and vicinity offered, be it long walks and brooks, or chained bears and vaudeville shows.

On the verandah, Columbia House, Hurleyville, New York, c. 1905. Manville Wakefield Collection

City guests flirted with small-town summer country life with nostalgic delight. But for many Catskill resort guests, escaping the city implied not only avoiding the foul air and congestion, but also

Nature domesticated for resort guests. Summit Hill House, Catskill, New York, c. 1900. The Bronck Museum Collection

avoiding contact with strangers. For "Old Americans," *strangers* meant *immigrants*. The same impulse which prompted a flight to the controlled private environment of the suburbs spurred some hotel guests to build their own private summer cottages and residential parks, such as Twilight Park and Onteora, established in the 1880s. Those guests who continued to go to public hotels and boarding houses also sought to preserve the "purity" of the setting with guests of a common social—gentile and American—background.

For all the simplicity and good will of vacation life, an ugly undercurrent of nativism and anti-Semitism ran through the summer hotels. In the 1880s, this erupted in blatant policies of exclusion, which survived in some resorts until World War II. Alice Hyerman Rhine, a progressive reformer, tried to analyze the source of "Race Prejudice at Summer Resorts" in 1887, and concluded,

> The existing state of acute antipathy owes its origin in part to a prevailing Christian ignorance concerning the Jews; partly, again, to the idle lives led during the summer season by frequenters of seaside and mountain resorts. In the absence of more entertaining topics,

THE VISTA,

Haines Falls, - Greene County, N. Y.

Convenient Railway, Mail and Telegraph communication. In the midst of the most important points of interest in the Catskills. At the head of the Kaaterskill Clove, on the Kaaterskill Railroad. Capacity for 50 Boarders. All appointments first-class. Altitude 2,000 feet. No Bar.

Terms: $8 to $10 per Week. $1.50 to $2 per Day for Transients.

JEWISH PEOPLE NOT RECEIVED.

Opposite Twilight and Sunset Parks. Extensive Golf Grounds near, all of which was formerly a part of Vista property.

OPEN FROM MAY 27, TO NOVEMBER 15.

MISS A. ELY, **Proprietress,**
Successor to S. P. Scott.

Exclusionary policies were blatantly advertised by some Catskill hotels until 1906 when New York State law made such overt discrimination illegal. *Ulster & Delaware Guide*, 1903, Evers Collection

"The Catskills offers its prodigal wealth to millionaires and to those of limited means alike." Kirk Munroe, *Summer in the Catskill Mountains,* 1883. Mohonk Mountain House and Sadie Kotler Collections

personalities are the staple of conversation. An inborn prejudice against the Jews brings the brunt of criticism to bear upon them.

The very increase of anti-Semitic feelings reflected the increase in the number of Jews going to Catskill resorts in the 1880s. Successful immigrants who sought to enjoy the trappings of their success found again and again such exclusionary notices as: "People not familiar with Catskills, know that except at the large hotels, the Jews and Gentiles will not generally board at the same house. This is to be regretted but being the fact, the houses have to take one class or the other. Therefore, the proprietor begs to say the Loxhurst accommodates Gentiles only."

Rhine noted that the anti-Semitic sentiment in Catskill resorts appeared most pronounced in the boarding houses, whose guests, relatively less secure about their own status, were consequently more hostile to outsiders. The larger hotels could maintain their class, if not their "ethnic purity," by their prices.

Many of the predominantly Jewish boarding houses which sprang up in the face of exclusion resembled their gentile counterparts in tone and style. In his 1917 novel, *The Rise of David Levinsky*, for example, Abraham Cahan has Levinsky — a successful clothing manufacturer—go to a Catskill hotel in the early 1900s, where he mingles with other Jews who have "made it" in the garment trades, as well as with guests of more modest standing. The guests, as Cahan describes them, pursued leisure with the same self-consciousness and material display that marked many of the nearby gentile establishments.

The bulk of the boarders at the Rigi Kulm were made up of families of cloak-manufacturers, cigar manufacturers, clothiers, furriers, jewelers, leather goods men, real estate men, physicians, dentists, lawyers, in most cases people who had blossomed into nabobs in the course of the last few years. The crowd was ablaze with diamonds . . . and bright colored silks. It was a babel of blatant self-consciousness, a miniature of the parvenu smugness that had spread like wild-fire over the country after a period of need and low spirits. In addition to families who were there for the whole season . . . the hotel contained a considerable number of single young people of both sexes — salesmen, stenographers, bookkeepers, librarians — who came for a fortnight's vacation. These were known as "two-weekers."

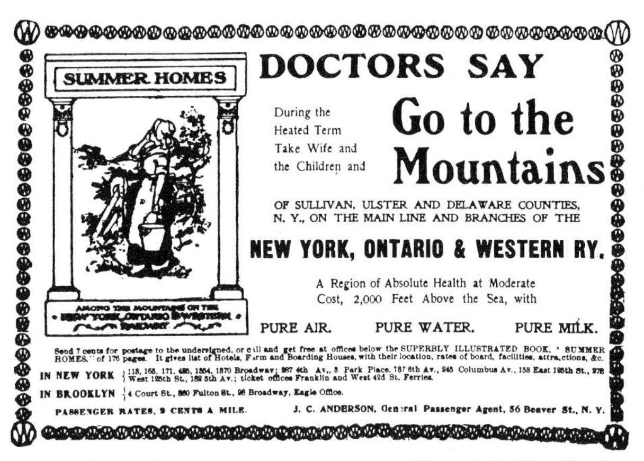

New York *Evening Post*, June 1, 1901, Manville Wakefield Collection

"This Grand Asylum"

"To the tired traveler, oppressed with heat and the burden of the day," an 1880s brochure announced, "the very approach of this grand asylum, provided by Mother nature for her fainting children, is an inspiration to new life. . . . The mountains promise rest." For some city dwellers, the image of fainting children and the promise of rest were more than mere rhetoric. In the years from 1890 to 1920, over ten million immigrants from Eastern and Southern Europe, Russia, Italy, and elsewhere came through the port of New York, settled in the metropolitan area, and went to work in the garment industry and at light manufacturing, food processing, and shopkeeping. The city's overcrowded housing and inadequate sanitation exacerbated the conditions which fed epidemics of tuberculosis, emphysema, and other lung diseases. In 1904 alone, over four thousand five hundred New York City residents died of tuberculosis.

In 1896, Dr. A. L. Loomis opened a tuberculosis sanitorium in the Catskills at Liberty. The Ontario and Western Railroad further encouraged New Yorkers to look to the mountains for cures by printing testimonials from doctors and by introducing guides to "winter homes" aimed specifically at consumptives. City dwellers were quick to develop a further mystique about the fresh food of the countryside, especially the wholesome milk, homemade cheese, and butter from "tuberculin-tested" cows.

For city immigrants, summers in the mountains became part of a collective strategy to preserve the physical, mental, and emotional well-being of their own community. Indeed, New York's Jewish population, with the lowest mortality rate of any ethnic group in the city, adopted the mountains as their own special clinic and resource. The high incidence of consumption prompted immigrant families to feel an urgency about getting their children out of the city for the summer months whenever possible. Families and individuals went by day steamer, train, and later by hired hacks and buses to the farms, kocheleins, boarding houses, and hotels, where they found people like themselves sharing and observing their own cultural traditions without the intrusions of the work world or city pressures to Americanize. Abraham Cahan's fictional David Levinsky conveys the sensation commonly experienced by guests who came from the Lower East Side:

> I had never been to the mountains before, nor practically never taken a day's vacation. It was so full of ozone, so full of health-giving balm, it was almost overpowering. I was inhaling it in deep, intoxicating gulps. It gave me a pleasure so keen it seemed to verge on pain. It was so unlike the air I had left in the sweltering city that the place seemed to belong to another planet.

Jewish families had begun settling in the Catskill valleys of Sullivan County during the 1890s. Such organizations as the Jewish Agricultural Society encouraged recent immigrants from Russia and Eastern Europe to move permanently into rural New York and New Jersey. Between 1900 and 1906, one article reported that Jewish families had purchased twelve hundred farms in the region around Ellenville alone. Families who tried farming often found that summer boarders brought in a more reliable income.

The first generation of Russian and Eastern European Jewish immigrants created a new form of Catskill boarding house: the kochelein ("cook-alone"). The kochelein dispensed with the high costs of service and hotel-catered meals. Each family brought its own linen and food supplies and shared a communal kitchen, with each mother doing her own family's cooking. Many people who grew up with kochelein summers recall the negotiations over kitchen space, refrigerator shelves, and stove burners which accompanied the accommodation of ten to twelve Jewish mothers in one room.

In a further effort to save money, some immigrant families who visited Catskill farms shared barrack-type quarters with curtain dividers, letting the expanse of the out-of-doors compensate for the multi-family crowding inside. Immigrants also called on the support of extended families in making summer trips. When working parents found it impossible to take their children to the mountains, other adult relatives, especially aunts and cousins who were themselves not working at the time, took the children of several families with them to a Catskill boarding house.

In the less orthodox Jewish boarding houses, women played cards when they were not keeping house and cooking, while children were left to explore on their own. At the more orthodox houses, women refrained from any organized amuse-

When they could, fathers joined their families at summer retreats. West Shokan Farm, Sullivan County, 1924. Sadie Kotler Collection

ments. Husbands and fathers came, when they could, for weekend visits. Comedian Joey Adams and others recall the transformation wrought by the anticipation and the arrival of the "husband train," which was often literally met at the station with a brass band. With the husbands' arrival, the resort took on a whole new aspect. Now it was men who were sitting on the verandah playing cards. Only occasionally did men join the family for the entire summer, and then usually because health dictated it or because they had been laid off for the season and found that country life was as cheap as remaining unemployed in the city. While Catskill resorts had always been intensely social environments, the kochelein, with its preeminent family focus, introduced a new dimension of communal living.

Though not to the same degree, other immigrant groups from the city also found the mountains a welcome retreat. One second-generation Italian recalls embarking on the day boat from Hoboken with his aunt and going to stay at a boarding house in Cairo where he missed his mother's spaghetti sauce. Each ethnic group had its own pattern of immigration and its unique family structure, with resulting differences in vacation habits. Italian immigrant populations included substantially fewer women and children than Eastern European Jewish groups in the first decades of the twentieth century, and the large proportion of Italians who planned to return to Italy meant that savings would be earmarked for return passages rather than a trip to the mountains. Given these and other cultural patterns, it was Jewish guests who came to dominate Sullivan County resort life.

Urban children raised within the summer tradition of "going to the mountains" retain vivid memories that range from distaste for the warm and all-too-fresh cow's milk to affection for the freedom they had to explore a new setting. As the *Brooklyn Eagle* commented, "there were no 'keep off the grass signs' and no vigilante-eyed 'coppers' to keep them from throwing pebbles or picking wild-flowers."

To extend the vacation opportunity to those who needed it most but could not afford private camps, benevolent societies began special summer-camp funds for city children. In the 1880s, the most famous of these, New York's Fresh Air Fund, was already sending nearly a hundred children to mountain homes each summer; by 1927, the Jewish philanthropic organizations sent more than nine thousand children per season to summer camp in Cold Spring. Perhaps the most significant camps to leave their mark on the mountains and on the memories of those who attended them were the

HUDSON RIVER BY DAYLIGHT.

A Choice of Two Routes to the

RESORTS OF THE CATSKILLS.

MUSIC! MUSIC!

The Two Fastest Boats in the World!

THE IRON PALACE STEAMERS

NEW YORK and ALBANY,

Leave New York—Vestry Street Pier, 8.40 A. M.; 22d Street Pier, N. R., 9 A. M. connecting at Rhinebeck (by ferry) with Express Trains on the

ULSTER & DELAWARE RAILROAD,

Giving a through connection for the Stony Clove & Catskill Mountain and Kaaterskill Railroads; also at CATSKILL with

CATSKILL MOUNTAIN RAILWAY.

Returning, close connection is made by both Routes with steamer for New York

ROUND TRIP TICKETS AT REDUCED RATES.

C. K. VAN BENTHUYSEN, *General Ticket Agent.* C. T. VAN SANTVOORD, *General Manager.*

Summer Excursions 1887, West Shore Railways, Evers Collection

Unity House, the summer camp of the ladies' garment workers, started at the once exclusive Overlook Mountain House in Catskill, New York. For labor and political groups, the mountains offered a retreat in which the fellowship of relaxation reinforced the solidarity of purpose. ILGWU *Yearbook*, Tamiment Library Collection.

Pioneer Youth Camps, founded in the early 1920s by trade unions of the garment industry, teachers, builders, machinists, firemen, and other city unions. The Pioneer Youth Camps introduced a tradition of progressive children's camps in which the children sitting around the campfire were as likely to discuss factory conditions and race prejudice as to hear nature lore or lectures on campcraft. Though they were emphatic about taking advantage of the natural setting, the camps also directed attention to the society in its larger sense.

A summer vacation was hardly within the reasonable range of expectation for most adult immigrant workers at the turn of the century. A 1909 *New York Times* survey asked a group of women in the garment trades to consider how much they would need to earn in order to save enough for a vacation. "They thrashed the matter out and decided that no girl earning less than $8.00 could possibly support herself and lay aside anything for the summer." Yet the average weekly wage for most of these women was $6.00. Reporting on the dilemma of vacations for "working girls," the same report went on to note that, contrary to the "pleasing delusion that the average shopgirl has her 4 or 5 dollars a week for pin money, a large number of them have to help their families." It concluded that of three hundred thousand "working girls in New York, only 6,783 obtain vacation outings through churches, settlements and societies devoted to that end." Ironically, the image of laboring women locked in airless sweatshops throughout the long hot summer appealed to the charitable impulses of many manufacturers who contributed to vacation societies. These same manufacturers did not, however, extend either their paternalism or their benevolence to their own workers as a regular policy. Clearly, there were few workers in the sweat trades who could afford excursions to the mountains for mere relaxation.

Though a railroad brochure pronounced the vacation habit "chronic and confirmed among all classes" by 1903, it was a selective habit. In 1910, when President Taft pronounced that every individual needed a vacation of several months' duration, *The New York Times* conducted a survey among "Big Employers of Labor and Men of Affairs" in order to determine the current public philosophy on vacations. The vice-president of the IRT subway spoke for a good number of his fellow employers when he remarked that "the value of a vacation depends upon how far you go down the line. I am a great believer in vacations and very liberal ones for men who work under mental strain. But it is different with the man whose work is merely physical work." Another railroad executive concurred, "The laboring man seems to be in a class by himself, so far as vacations are concerned. ... Many corporations now hire this force under hourly wage agreements and it is rare that a man has a full year's work. The result is that the time 'off,' owing to changing conditions, takes the place of a vacation, but of course at their own expense."

One of the few "men of affairs" to advocate the principle of vacations for workers and management alike, Supreme Court Justice Henry Bischoff, concluded, "Then too, I believe that the laboring man ought to get a vacation, but unfortunately he cannot unless he takes it—and then it is without pay which means a lot to him, you know." In the prewar twentieth century, the very concept of a vacation as a basic right for workers struck bosses as an unreasonable luxury.

Vacations for those who worked at "mental labor," however, became increasingly common. In 1916, the federal government instituted a paid-vacation policy for all civil-service employees. During the twenties, private employers interested in "scientific management" gradually began to realize that worker morale was a component of worker productivity. Expanding on this enlightened new perspective, one article demonstrated the benefits of vacations by noting: "Who gains? The employee gains directly in their getting a better body and mind to work with, and the employer by thus improving the morale and increasing efficiency of the co-workers. Such employers are rarely troubled with anyone striking." Still, by 1930 only 10 to 15 percent of the industrial labor force in the United States had paid summer vacations.

Even without paid vacations, labor unions in New York City had long drawn on the accessibility and relative economy of Catskill resorts to promote and subsidize workers' retreats. The International Ladies Garment Workers Union, especially, undertook special summer vacation programs for "working girls," men, and their children. With time and space away from their work and the surveillance that accompanied it, workers could reflect on their situation and organize their resistance against long hours, subsistence wages, and oppressive working conditions. In addition to the unions, both the Socialist and Communist parties held organizing and planning meetings at Catskill hotels throughout the twenties and the thirties, and the labor and left-wing tradition of adult and youth camps survives today. The mountains offer a retreat in which the fellowship of relaxation reinforces the solidarity of purpose.

Cars, Camps, and Country Clubs: The Social Scene Accelerates

As New York's Jewish population prospered and moved out of the city to the cleaner air of Long Island, the Bronx, and Brooklyn, the Catskill resorts at which they vacationed were also expanding and prospering. Kosher boarding houses and farmhouses which had put up an average of twenty to fifty guests during the first two decades of the twentieth century now grew to provide accommodations for from one hundred to three hundred.

For Catskill guests, the 1920s and 1930s opened the era of organized, man-made recreational facilities, formal schedules of activities, and informal manners. A new style of fun and a new aura of personal freedom accompanied the new prosperity of many resort guests; at the same time, the mountain resorts continued to affirm the traditional values of family and shared culture, however secular their form and expression.

The composition of the resorts changed dramatically between 1925 and 1950. As agriculture declined, and as the clinical cure of the mountains lost its urgency, many of the smaller, more marginal boarding-house and farmhouse resorts closed down. More conspicuously, the grand hotels of the railroad era also closed and often burned—while their wealthy former guests pursued more exotic vacations in Europe or Florida, or more exclusive ones in private summer homes. The Catskills disappeared from the summer social notes of *The New York Times* as gentile social elites continued to refuse to mix with Jewish guests. At the same time, as many of those Jewish guests themselves grew more prosperous, they moved from boarding-house resorts to their own new luxury hotels.

Indeed, many of the boarding houses either expanded into hotel buildings or built their own additional wings. In 1914, Grossinger's, the archetypal Catskill resort, moved from its original farmhouse to a previously gentile hotel building and began adding rooms. When guests overflowed the already built premises, many proprietors of similar resorts simply put the guests in tents. In Sullivan County, whole new towns and resort clusters developed in the 1920s—Kiamesha Lake, Swan Lake, and Loch Sheldrake.

The tremendous boom in hotel building and expansion alarmed some observers. In 1924, a writer in the *Jewish Farmer* summed up the transformation: "Whither are we going? It is some ten or fifteen years now that the expansion has been going on in every direction without a halt or let up. All the time new houses are being built and old ones remodelled. Unpretentious farm houses are giving place to huge monsters of brick and mortar."

The "monsters" were more frequently of stucco, and their construction continued to flourish throughout the twenties. A hotel for as many as three hundred guests had been an exception in the railroad era, but large hotels now became the rule in Sullivan County. They were not, however, the only type. In the well-established tradition of the Catskills, resorts operated on several economic tiers.

Large hotels, catering to new wealth, dubbed themselves "country clubs," with all the connotations of suburban luxury. Like the clubs, these hotels stressed their recreational facilities as well as the high status of their clientele. At the other end of the economic scale, bungalow colonies and adult camps, following in the tradition of communal kocheleins, added new gloss and vigor to the more economic summer retreat. The camps appealed especially to second-generation young adults — often college students or beginning professionals — whose prosperity awaited the further advancement of their careers. Bungalow colonies continued to serve those middle-income families who had not accumulated large savings but who nonetheless earned enough to afford two weeks away from the city.

The proliferation of activities required a schedule and a social director to achieve the well-managed vacation. *Vacation Guide*, New York, Ontario & Western Railway, 1933, Barbara Purcell Collection

In the 1920s, the pace of resort life altered dramatically, and the automobile was both the vehicle and the symbol for the change in style. The chauffeur-driven autos and elite "coaching parties" of the early 1900s gave way to hackney cabs, buses, and the Model T. Cars gave new mobility to the individual families who could afford them, and eased general access through their collective use. Hotels, hackney companies, and private entrepreneurs started regular runs between the cities and the mountains. The new convenience and independence extended to vacation life as well. Even more than the informal outdoors and hiking clothes which women had adopted during the 1880s and 1890s, the outfit and the "look" of the 1920s motoring woman endorsed and encouraged an active and a mobile life.

Hotels took advantage of the new trend by ceasing to advocate vacations for serene contemplation, health, and rest, and they joined the resort pages of newspapers in celebrating activities, especially organized athletics. No longer could the large resorts simply incorporate the natural setting into their grounds—a lawn for tennis, a lake for swimming, or a field for baseball. The athletics of the twenties required prepared terrains; and to be complete in the eyes of their sports-minded vacationers, the hotels were impelled to add swimming pools, clay tennis courts, and, where they could afford them, golf courses. Basketball courts and handball courts introduced the urban sports terrain as well. Those guests with money adopted the Catskill resort as their own country club away from home, while the traditional boarding-house verandah and lawn receded in prominence to serve only those for whom the fresh air alone still offered a welcomed contrast to the city.

Prohibition heightened the clublike atmosphere of many of the resorts. Although Jewish guests were seldom heavy drinkers, the Catskill counties assumed public notoriety for bootlegging action. The pace accelerated even for children, as Catskill guests began to socialize with new energy and freedom. One newspaper reported that

> there was a movement some time ago to have children barred from the dance halls which cover much of this summer recreation ground. The reason assigned was that this was to conserve the morals. The real reason — the natives frankly tell you — is that the children when taken to dances by their parents or older relatives were under instruction to prowl the premises, and when couples were dancing to sneak under the table and steal bottles they might have left behind.

The new generation that came of age following World War I had had its precursors in earlier gen-

“In the evening . . . there is a dance. The young people assemble, the musicians (college undergraduates) appear . . . and the wailing history of red hot mama’s high frequency vies with the drone of mosquitoes.” *New York Times,* August 11, 1929. Sugar Maples, Maplecrest, New York

erations, for more than one elegant hotel in the eighties had contrasted its serenity with what were called the “low frivolities and wearying carousings of so many of our resorts.” But it was not until the 1920s that resort activity acquired both a regular schedule and a distinctive motif: the camp. Keynoting the era, Loch Sheldrake Rest announced “The REST is meeting the requirements of the Time. It shall be conducted as a modern CAMP in every respect. A noted social director shall provide entertainment in the morning, afternoon, and evening.”

The schedule came to rule resort life during the 1920s and 1930s, though often “schedule” meant simply a regimen of what actually amounted to the same old activities. One 1929 reporter deplored the relatively hectic new pace by observing that “efficiency enslaves the summer boarders; joy lives by the clock at Camp Legion.” Yet the activities he went on to describe included the familiar blackberry-picking expedition, the four-o’clock swim, and the evening dance. In his autobiography, Moss Hart, recalling his days as a Catskill camp social director, describes the schedule for every night of the week: it ranged from campfires to basketball, from masquerade nights to musical comedy performances. During the day, at least one resort in 1931 advertised, “something doing every minute,” a promise echoed with only slightly more restraint thirty years later by the Concord’s boast of “something happening every hour.” In theory, scheduled activity offered guests not simply entertainment, but the best means for meeting other guests. For its apologists, the schedule existed in order to coordinate the socializing, but for its opponents, the schedule was simply another instrument of social control.

Resort time, though paced differently than the routine of work, had never been entirely free of structure. Boarding houses always had ordered life by rigidly fixed meal hours around which guests planned their days. One brochure advised, “Parties can walk past the Glen and Moses Walk to the Catskill Mountain House after breakfast and return by dinner time.” Yet it was not until the twentieth century that resorts introduced systematic planning of activities within the day’s schedule.

In hotels and boarding houses where the same guests returned year after year, informal entertainments—dances, concerts, lectures—acquired the casing of “tradition.” Everyone at Mohonk even today knows that the fossil hunt is on Sunday afternoon, and the proprietor of the Bavarian Manor maintains the tradition of the “mock wedding” every Thursday night. The distinction between tradition and schedule collapsed when new vacationers coming for a shorter stay “had to be told” the customs of the house.

The most important feature of both camps and country clubs was the social director. Claiming descendance from the Jewish “tumlers” (tumult makers), social directors inherited not only their traditional wit and the role of entertaining guests, but the fuller responsibility of attempting to guarantee the happiness of the assembled community. Hotel staffs, too, ceased to provide mere service and concentrated on entertainment, with college-bound waiters and waitresses doubling as musicians, actors, and comedians. For that select class of social directors who became professional entertainers, from Moss Hart to Danny Kaye, a season in the Catskills in the 1920s and 1930s provided rigorous training in stamina, imagination, and tolerance.

Staffs and guests put together weekly shows ranging from skit nights to full-fledged musical comedy productions. Moss Hart's autobiography recalls the frenetic pace, the spontaneity, and the talent that made the Catskill summer theatricals legendary among those who later moved on to Hollywood, Broadway, and television. The resorts continue to cherish the stars and impresarios who came out of the mountains, from Lenny Bruce and Bill Graham to Joel Grey. Some of the star entertainers in their turn have "gone back" to the mountains, appearing on widely advertised weekends at resorts where they first appeared as fledglings. As theater became a major drawing card for guests during the 1920s, hotels began to expand their entertainment facilities as well as their professional entertainment staffs. At the end of the twenties, Hart became social director of the Flagler Hotel, which had just built a theater to accommodate fifteen hundred people — not only its own guests, but those of the adjacent resort neighborhood as well.

The Catskill youth and young-adult camps of the 1920s, unlike many of the traditional children's camps, were emphatically co-ed. And, far from seeking to inculcate the sense of responsibility that informed the Pioneer Youth or Fresh Air Fund camps of the area, young-adult camps (for those from sixteen to thirty) fostered whatever degrees of irresponsibility the campers and staff could get away with. Indeed, one ex-camper recalls with distaste the constant promotion of courtship that dominated camp life. Appropriately, Marjorie Morningstar's mother was later to dub such camps "Sodom."

Courting is an ancient theme of Catskill resort life. Charles Baldwin graphically recorded in his 1860s diary the pleasure of his day trip to the Kaaterskill Falls in the company of several eligible women.

> As my carriage was not wide enough for three on the seat, I sat on the laps of my two friends, and drove. They put their arms around me, which pleased me very much. At the several bridges I collected "toll" from each of them in the shape of a kiss. Part of the time friend Sarah sat on my lap and drove: while I put one arm around her waist to steady her, and the other arm around friend Lizzie. . . . The whole party was in excellent spirits, and we had much fun during the whole drive.

Another resort-goer of that earlier period also remarked on the freedom from the restraints and ceremonials of city life which allowed men and women alike a freedom of movement and activity often suppressed in the parlors of Victorian homes. But as those resorts expanded their own parlors and verandahs, freedom from the surveillance of watchful mothers sometimes became harder to secure.

The husband-hunting resort mother became famous early in the canons of Catskill literature. As rather kindly described in 1899 by James Ford, "such a woman has her daughters always on her mind, and feels that she should take them to some place where there is 'something going on,' as she would express it, signifying an opportunity for them to make desirable acquaintances and perhaps to encounter some eligible young men who would make good husbands."

The preponderance of women at Catskill resorts stemmed in large part from the structure of work and the social conventions of the middle class. In the late ninteenth century, those women employed as teachers, for example, had their summers free. And the great majority of women who were not employed depended on finding a husband to secure their futures. Furthermore, the common social wisdom of many reformers advocated summer vacations for "working girls" and encouraged them

Part of the "young crowd" at the Sunrise Hotel, Livingston Manor, 1949. Gladys and Bernard Leon Collection

to go to the mountains. What remains most interesting about the Catskills as a mating ground is the confidence of resort-goers that other guests share enough of the same cultural background, values, and "suitable" economic status to share a life as well. The role of resort prejudice and ethnic exclusion becomes more complex when perceived as a strategy to preserve the cultural integrity of particular religious and ethnic groups.

Women often found that the "opportunity" was vastly overrated. One woman who recalls going to a small hotel in Livingston Manor with her parents during the thirties remembers that "you always met boys. Always the waiters would go after the girls. I met a waiter and dated him when I got back to New York. But when I came home, he wasn't nearly so interesting. Always, it was more exciting in the mountains."

Though resort waiters may not have stood up under the scrutiny of city lights, hotels employed college students as waiters and staff precisely to guarantee the summer's romantic quotient to their guests. The family resort implicitly testified to suitability and the future earning power of its staff, even though it could not always vouch for moral rectitude. Many a hotel romance brought couples back to the mountains for free honeymoons or family vacations years later.

The romancing in the mountains became a favorite theme of humorists such as playwright Arthur Kober, who satirized camp life and suggested some of the complications:

TEDDY: Her husband here with her?

FAY: Nah! He oney comes down week-ends.

MIRIAM: But this week-end he hadda be detained by business.

FAY: *(knowingly)*. That's what he said!

MIRIAM: So what has she got to do but go after the single boys?

FAY: Some of the married women here are so common, you got no idear.

MIRIAM: And the boys like the married women. One or two of them are positively wild!

TEDDY: *(the smart conversationalist)*. If their husbands only knew! *(She goes off to bathroom)*.

MIRIAM: *(with a sign of resignation)*. Well, that's what we got to contend with here at camp. Trouble enough finding a nice serious type boy without some flighty married woman snatching him away.

A Family Affair

Through a century of changing vacation styles and changing guests, the Catskill resorts have maintained a remarkable resilience. The mixture and growth of resorts have responded to and reflected the varying economic conditions of their guests. Because of their location, the resorts have also thrived during period of economic stress, from the depression of 1893, through the Great Depression of the thirties, and beyond it into the uneasy present. The rhythm of openings and expansions, closings and fires, has been uninterrupted since the beginning.

The economic prosperity of the 1920s prompted guests to desert the Catskills in favor of more glamorous destinations: the luxury hotels of the railroad era were all too familiar and set all too close to home to compete with the siren calls of suddenly affordable Florida, California, and Europe in the twenties. For some guests, Catskill hotels had also become too "strange" with the advent of immigrant guests. The same automobile which made it more convenient to get away to the mountains, also freed those tourists who might previously have traveled by train or day boat to the Catskills. Offsetting these desertions, however, was the discovery of the mountain resorts by newly successful city dwellers and immigrants. Thus new levels of prosperity have repeatedly introduced a new population of guests even as they drew away the old. As many of Greene County's grand hotels closed down, the boarding houses of Sullivan County expanded into newer and more contemporary versions of those hotels.

Not all the Catskill resorts adopted the camp motif in the twenties and thirties. Some, such as Thompson House and Mohonk, stressed a policy of nonintervention, leaving their guests to structure their own time and activity. One result was that such traditional hotels often suffered in competition with the modern country clubs. By the mid-twentieth century, the social life of Catskill resorts had triumphed over Nature, and the large activities-oriented hotels dominated the mountains. The resort landscape offered less in the way of a retreat from the city than an instant community of friends and extended family in a different setting.

In Sullivan County, resorts continued to expand their organized recreation and live entertainment as though to concentrate all the benefits of the new leisure into one place to be enjoyed at one time. Many resorts shifted from being "summer homes" marked by the leisurely pace of an extended stay to being the "vacation," a special time and place for consuming a year's worth of fun. Yet the resorts remained vulnerable to the passing of time and the fluctuations of the larger economy. The thirties were a period of sharp retrenchment.

Hotels have developed specific strategies for times of economic depression. In the thirties, fore-

Twentieth-century Catskill guests vigorously continue to pursue health and relaxation in the mountains. Lakeside Inn, Sullivan County, 1944. Manville Wakefield Collection

closures and fires decimated the number of Catskill hotels, eliminating especially the small boarding house, and many of the larger "country clubs" as well. With over three million people out of work and millions of others taking wage cuts, money for a vacation was a luxury beyond contemplation for most Americans. Those resorts which survived did so by lowering their rates and sharply cutting their staffs. The grand hotel of Mohonk, which lost half its guests, kept its staff in exchange for board alone and weathered the Depression with sheer Yankee obstinacy and Quaker fortitude. Still, Karl Bauer opened the Bavarian Manor just after the crash, Grossinger's installed its first golf course in the early thirties, and Arthur Winarick transformed the old Kiamesha Lake Lodge into the new Concord in 1937.

Summer air did not improve in the City just because no one had any money to get very far away from it. Those Depression guests with any savings who might have traveled farther and for longer during the twenties, returned to the mountains in the thirties. Similarly, owner-built bungalow colonies (organized as kocheleins) and adult camps offered economy vacations for young people. One "camper" recalls going for two weeks to a Catskill adult camp where most of his friends worked as waiters, a still lucrative summer job for college students.

For those willing to take the risk and able to raise the money, the buildings of expired hotels stood ready to be revived and reincarnated. As highway building continued with New Deal Public Works, automobile access to the mountains was growing even easier. The New York State Thruway opened in 1938. As the Depression ended the life of one generation of Catskill resorts, it consolidated the strengths of the new generation of country-club hotels, which accommodated from three hundred to over five hundred guests by 1940, and were still growing.

As much as access to the great eastern cities, it is family proprietorship and guest loyalty that have created the unique character and contributed to the survival of Catskill resorts. Many hotels now moving toward a third, fourth, or even fifth generation in the same family have weathered rocky economic periods on the strength of a combination of equity and personal savings, an extended-family labor force, and the financial and moral support of relatives and friends. Proprietors have not easily relinquished those resorts which are not only their businesses, but their homes. Similarly, loyal guests have not quickly abandoned resorts which have also become part of the rhythm of their own family lives: the dependable regularity of its returning guests has seen many a resort through periods of stress.

As it did to other sectors of the economy, World War II brought recovery to the Catskill resort industry. Once again the accessibility of the mountains attracted vacationers who could simply get no farther on rationed gas. Whatever the constraints of rationing, the hotels advertised, there were "No priorities on fun, no rationing on Pleasure" in the mountains. And there were special rates for "men in uniform."

The ethnic diversity that we associate with the

Catskills today largely awaited the economic recovery and "normalization" of domestic life in the late forties and early fifties. After World War II, "new" ethnic groups discovered the mountains — Germans, more Italians, Armenians, Syrians, Hungarians, Greeks, French, and Irish. Certain towns and areas acquired specific ethnic identities: the "Borscht Belt" of Sullivan County with its grand Jewish resorts and bungalow colonies of South Fallsburg and Liberty; the "German Alps" of Hunter Mountain; the "Italian Alps" of Cairo, and the Irish strip of East Durham. Other groups scattered through the northern Catskills of Green County. In the late 1940s, one travel brochure for Haines Falls alone listed resorts with at least ten different cuisines — the unmistakable symbols of specific ethnic enclaves in the mountains.

As in city neighborhoods, there is a tradition of ethnic succession in the mountains. Just as Grossinger's adopted a formerly gentile boarding house when it first began to expand in the twenties, so Villa Maria has been Italian for only eighteen years; before that, its buildings served a Jewish clientele for seventeen years. The Mathe in Fleischmanns began during the forties as an Austrian and German resort; today it increasingly serves Hungarians and Armenians. Advertising in ethnic papers, and the even more reliable tactic of word of mouth, spread the news about exactly where visitors could plan to relax with others of their ethnic background.

The Suburban Wilderness

Over the past twenty-five years, the Sullivan County "palaces" have grown into small kingdoms, but many other hotels have struggled with problems ranging from obsolescence to the incipient ice age. Those hotels which have aggressively sought to diversify their clientele — courting conventions, "singles," and other special-interest groups — have continued to expand. Others remain vulnerable and dependent on the loyalties of guests who have grown up with summers in the mountains, and who love Catskill life for exactly those qualities which make it too prosaic and predictable to vacationers who want quick stimulation and change. In some sense, the history of the resorts in the last twenty-five years has reflected the larger history of a particular generation: those who came of age during the twenties and thirties, started families during the late forties, grew successful and moved to the suburbs during the fifties, and in the sixties and seventies either continued going to the mountains or abandoned them, depending on their personal life stories.

As the 1950s began, many of the hotels of the southern Catskills were moving into a new era of growth and of competition. Seeking to identify and attract new clientele, resorts appealed directly to the "young crowd" who had begun going to the mountains as children. Indeed, the "crowd" at different hotels soon became one of their defining attributes. One couple recall visiting Cooks Falls Lodge in 1948, when they were in their mid-twenties and had just recently married: "We stayed there for two nights and we checked out and went back to the Sunrise again. Cooks Falls Lodge was an older crowd. . . . To make the air circulate better they had taken the glass out of the transoms, so you couldn't make any noise." (That same year Kutsher's was announcing "air conditioning in every room of [the] new Delux House," heralding the age of artificially cooled summer comfort.)

One selling feature of Catskill resorts during the 1950s was the opportunity to enjoy, for a week or two, this still-new standard of comfort and ease. If in the 1880s resorts had invited their guests to imagine themselves proprietors of country estates, in the 1950s the large hotels represented to them an ideal of suburban convenience. For young families who could not yet afford them, there were the luxuries of television, air-conditioning, wall-to-wall carpeting, separate dressing rooms, on-the-premises swimming pools, patios, queen-size beds, and privacy. Rustic nature faded even farther into the background as the hotels focused increasingly on their interiors and extra luxuries. The enormous interest in convenience and improvements was a blow to the older boarding houses and resorts which could not secure funding for extensive renovation and new buildings. And few resorts could match the Concord's 1962 announcement of rooms with king-size beds and two baths each.

As part of the new ease, as well as part of the suburban family ideal, resorts undertook to provide for the children, "to take them off the hands of relaxing parents." Children had never been fully integrated into the country-club resort, and their subsequent incorporation into resort life was not always easy. While some hotels simply ruled out children altogether, others tried to hide their ambivalence. The Wildemere described itself in 1962 as "The Only Happy Place for Adults Only," while the Grand Hotel in the fifties had advertised for "COUPLES with a CHILD or two," suggesting that perhaps the day-camp staff was not prepared to deal with large sibling conspiracies. By the 1950s, the vast majority of the large hotels had introduced new facilities for children and had begun advertising the "Parent-Child Resort."

The informing principle of the "Parent-Child Resort" was that separate-but-equal facilities led to the greatest happiness for the greatest number, and that parents were more equal than children. Many

In the 1950s, many Catskill hotels developed special age-group programs as part of the "separate but together" family vacation.
Grossinger's, Grossinger, New York

larger hotels developed elaborate child-care programs with in-house day camps, bed checks, separate dining rooms, and even teen-age nightclubs. Parents could enjoy themselves knowing that their children were well provided for; and children had the relief of separation from parental authority. While many parents and children who went to these hotels found the scheme to be in the interest of all parties, at least one disgruntled former child guest claims that the company of peers with whom she was placed was not nearly as much fun as her parents would have been. And more than one of the large hotels today has trouble persuading the children to stay down at the day camp when the real excitement seems to be up at the house.

Many large resorts continue to advertise "separate vacations . . . together" and "the children are off in a world of their own," but others try to create a vacation environment in which children and adults can play and enjoy themselves together. Villa Maria and Winter Clove offer special entertainment for the children, but most of their adult and child guests join together in the activities of swimming, boccie, athletics, and the nightclubs. Indeed, one Italian mother explained that she had selected Villa Maria over a swank resort up the road precisely because its family atmosphere kept the children in the center of activity. Nevertheless, resorts such as Villa Maria—which accommodates three generations with the ease of a house in Brooklyn—are unusual. The trend in larger hotels encourages the separation of children and adolescents from their parents, and fewer and fewer families choose to spend a summer vacation in the mountains. In contrast to the general decline of family vacations, many older people now living on their own continue to go to the mountain resorts they visited thirty years ago. The children of the postwar baby boom are growing older, and the care of children at many resorts has receded as a major issue. But as already mature guests grow older, attracting new, younger guests remains a challenge.

If the musical comedy was the paradigm of entertainment in the twenties and the thirties, in the fifties and the sixties, entertainment became the nightclub act *cum* television special. The shift from staff entertainment to circuit road shows focused attention less on a whole production than on individual performers, especially comedians or singers. Low lighting and bandstands transformed playhouses, casinos, and social halls into cocktail lounges and nightclubs. And, as had been true for over a hundred years, after the show was over the band played on for dancing. The war brought a significant change to the style of resort entertainment. With much of the traditional workforce of young waiters in the service, hotels cut back on staff entertainment and increasingly relied on the solitary performer. In any case, guests who returned every summer to the same hotels grew tired of predictable routines and shows and seemed to welcome the variety of performers on circuit. The Sullivan County hotels increasingly relied on the Borscht Belt circuit to provide a different entertainer every week, and Friday and Saturday nights featured the really big entertainment. As in the years of day trippers to the Mountain House, guests at smaller neighboring hotels often tried to get in to the larger ones for the show. For a celebrity-conscious public, resorts found that the spectacle and glamour of famous entertainers and sports stars carried as much appeal as the guarantee of participation and constant activity.

In the forties, resorts had stressed their nonspecific "Broadway casts" and "radio artists." By the fifties, they began listing the celebrities singly as featured performers. Indeed, with the free publicity of television for stars, resorts became increasingly big-name conscious, seeking to associate themselves with particular names. ("And you open at Brown's on the sixteenth, right, Jerry?" "That's right, Johnny.")

Sports introduced another form of celebrity spectatorship. In the twenties, resorts had featured tournaments with golf and tennis pros to attract public attention. Olympic skaters and swimmers also added class to the pools and rinks. Grossinger's launched another phase of celebrity watching at resorts by inviting boxer Barney Ross to train at the hotel during the thirties. In one of the most famous moves toward spectatorship, Sullivan County hotels organized an intramural basketball circuit which achieved nationwide attention—and notoriety—by introducing amateur players into a game for money.

Meanwhile, smaller boarding houses and hotels have adapted to some of these trends, with nightclub entertainment on the weekends, local bands and dancing at their casinos during the week, and both staff and guest talent shows. At Scott's, the

During the 1920s, Catskill resorts and guests brought "urban" sports to the countryside, and waiters added basketball to their other extensive activities. *Vacation Guide*, New York, Ontario & Western Railway, 1937, Barbara Purcell Collection

family quite literally maintains the tradition of the host entertaining guests. At the other extreme, in 1969 the Woodstock festival introduced the Catskills' largest open-air resort with all entertainment and no hotel.

The Present: Backyard Mountain

One nineteenth-century visitor to the Catskills, contemplating the relation of the resorts to the mountains, concluded, "But most of us are really only shopkeepers, and natural spectacles are but shop windows on a great scale. People love the country theoretically, as they do poetry." The modern resorts of the Catskills continue to draw on urban nostalgia for the countryside even as the resorts, rather than the mountains, supply the spectacle.

Twentieth-century guests have perhaps no less affection for the mountains, but they have had increasingly less contact since the time resorts first began socializing nature with their hiking trails, coaching roads, and with strategically situated gazebos and verandah-framed views. Swimming pools, golf courses, and ski lifts over artificial snow have superseded the old ponds and tannery roads. Like the architecture of modern resort hotels, the guests themselves have turned inward, away from the view. One proprietor brought the mountain back to his guests by simply transplanting the native mountain shrubs and trees to the hotel grounds. At another hotel, guests sit on city park benches to enjoy watching the steady stream of traffic to the pool. Although the contemporary revival of outdoors and campcraft sports is sending more and more visitors back into the mountains, the Catskills remain an eminently civilized wilderness.

The very terms of "civilization" in the Catskills have changed. As cities reach farther and farther toward their peripheries, the Catskills have become the backyard of New York, New Jersey, and eastern Pennsylvania, the familiar—almost prosaic—extension of middle-class urban recreational spheres. Today the hotels promote spectatorship and celebrate the skills of professionals, even as they encourage personal fitness and supply a ready guest audience of their own to applaud amateur skill, effort, or at least good intention. The resorts continue to offer leisure activity primarily as a vehicle for socializing, but more and more of their guests are people who want to take advantage of the concentration of facilities and only incidentally to interact with other guests.

The most serious disease which requires a mountain cure today is hay fever, though city guests continue to experience a shock with the first inhalation of fresh mountain air. The country weekend is the new unit of cure for the burdens of the work world and the harassment of city traffic. Lest time go unfilled, resorts have increasingly offered programs of instruction, or even programs of "experience" to entertain and edify their transient guests and give them something special to carry back to the city. Indeed, the resorts continue to seek out and supply that crucial ingredient still missing from home settings so that guests will rely on the mountains to fulfill needs created by the very opportunity for leisure and comfort.

As the "mini-vacation" has supplanted the summer stay, the resorts have lost their intimacy for many guests. Some patterns still survive, and many people who have a regular summer vacation scheduled at the same time every year continue to meet their "mountain friends" for the same week summer after summer. Meanwhile, the resorts themselves widely advertise the special "packages" they have developed for short vacations, which feature a common interest among guests, be it chamber music, environmental reform, or est. There are other guests who travel to the mountains with their own local interest groups, from the lodge or synagogue congregation to a mah-jong or retirement group. In contrast to these informal conventions of friends, neighbors, and relatives, the hotels have accelerated their efforts to attract formal conventions of businesses and social organizations, a long-time mainstay of the hotel industry in the mountains.

While some hotels perpetuate the tradition of recreating ethnic neighborhoods, others have moved toward assimilation. For some would-be guests, the pronounced ethnicity of the Catskill resorts has been a source of embarrassment, a condition to be left behind in the acquisition of mainstream American values and tastes. For others, ethnicity sustains and reaffirms common cultural heritage and identity. The two responses become more confused as ethnicity has become an American media event. One social director explained that he brought his children to a Catskill Italian resort for the summer "so that they wouldn't lose touch," and he laughed when the theme from *The Godfather* drifted from the teen game room. Many guests still frequent ethnic resorts because that is, after all, where their friends, neighbors, and families go. But as larger hotels direct their operations toward an anonymous and interchangeable American guest list to broaden their appeal, they often dilute exactly those ethnic qualities which once positively identified them.

To further the contradictions, some hotels feature ethnicity as part of the spirit of getting away from the routine and familiar settings of home life. At places such as the Bavarian Manor, the pro-

The singles weekender and the encounter group became fixtures at some hotels during the 1960s as resorts sought to attract younger guests. Grossinger's, Grossinger, New York

prietors contrive their atmosphere out of ethnic décor and cuisine which no longer carry an authentic tie to the cultural heritage that they evoke. Where in the early years of the twentieth century, the International Ladies Garment Workers Union of necessity served separate dinners to Italian and Jewish workers in the same camp dining room, today eating ethnic is as much a choice as a custom.

Diluted or not, the ethnic identity of the hotels remains part of their essential character, as well as the basis for Catskill humor. At Irish Gavin's Golden Hill and the Italian Villa Maria, part of the comfort still comes from sharing the pleasantries and manners of people of common backgrounds. And those hotels which maintain kosher kitchens can count on, at least for the immediate future, a guest list for whom traditional practices retain meaning and value. Resorts such as Mohonk, which holds religious services on the premises, echo the sentiment expressed nearly a century ago by a guest who found it simultaneously "a resort, a church, and a home."

Not one of the least significant ironies of the Catskills today is that the dichotomy between Jewish and gentile has given way to sharper distinctions between "modern" and "traditional," and between large and small. Thus Grossinger's and Mohonk, each the examplar of its kind, perhaps share more in common with each other in tone and effect than either does with less "orthodox" resorts. The blatantly advertised policies of exclusion have gone, leaving in their place a tacit agreement that people vacation in settings in which they feel at home.

Local Catskills tradition insists on the myth of the spontaneous generation of boarding houses out of the hospitality of farmhouses, as indeed it often sees their demise in spontaneous combustion. Native farmers, migrants to the region, and outside investors all built the Catskill resorts. In the nineteenth century, "outside" capital flowed from the transportation industry—from coaching companies, steamboats, and the railroads. But with the arrival of the car, sources of outside capital shifted to all-too-often uncooperative banks, and to private investment networks of friends and family. As many of the hotels have expanded, the demand for improved facilities with the increased requirements for capital have introduced the corollary of intense competition for guests.

Many resort proprietors understand the need for cooperation among the resorts to promote the region, but smaller resorts continue to be most vulnerable to the fluctuations in the economy, to competition, and to the everchanging tastes of resort-goers. The capacities of the larger hotels allow them to draw the lucrative convention trade and to monopolize many of the regional festivals and entertainments, while smaller hotels and resorts must depend on the attractions of their very size, and on the loyalty and the communal leanings of their guests.

Meanwhile, all the Catskill resorts have turned away from the community of the towns and villages. Though the ethnic festivals herald a new trend toward socializing among the hotels, each resort maintains its self-sufficiency today with sometimes belligerent pride. The railroad era's symbiotic relation between local dairy farms and the resorts has given way to the importation of both food and labor. During the Depression many a hotel which survived extended meager employment to local residents in exchange for board. But as contemporary full-fledged industries, today's resorts must either compete with the relatively high wage scales of other plants—such as IBM in New Paltz—or simply draw their labor from afar.

The most dramatic change in the resorts' internal organization has developed with the expansion and specialization of their staffs with the extension of "the season." When hotels ran on three-to-five-month summer seasons, they relied on students for labor. The students themselves were considered the "children" of the guests, and it was not unusual for staff and guests to mix socially, as did the "host"-proprietors and guests. Members of the resort communities grew sometimes painfully familiar with one another's peculiar habits, special talents, and personal histories. Even in the early years of the resorts, larger hotels also drew on a migrant hotel labor force which followed the season north in the spring. As the Catskill resorts themselves moved to a year-round season—starting in the thirties—and expanded their premises and their services, they turned to a regular year-round staff of hotel workers, and they continued to employ students only for the busy summer months. No longer was a guest's handsome waiter a prospective doctor; he was, instead, simply a handsome waiter. As a consequence, the class lines were more firmly drawn: the distance between host, guest, and staff has grown progressively greater in the larger hotels, recasting the flexible roles of earlier social life into the rigid and impersonal boundaries of employers and employees, management and customer.

Although the mountains have long been a vacation haven for the members of city unions, unions for workers in the resort business itself have not come easily to the mountains. The corrupt underside of Catskill resort life — the poor housing provided for workers, the more subtle hierarchies of staff social relations, status, and responsibility, the tensions between family and professional management, and the not-so-subtle hierarchies of tips and bribes — this presents a very different story about seasons in the mountains.

Of whatever size the establishment, it is the tradition of the family business that remains the most distinctive characteristic of the Catskill resort industry. Within the family tradition, however, more and more members of the second and third generations are inheriting not a family hotel, but interest in a family corporation; today they receive their training not at the check-out desk, or bussing in the dining room, but at hotel-management schools.

Much of the feeling of continuity in the mountain resorts still comes from perennial guests such as those at the Sugar Maples, who can qualify to inscribe their names in concrete after twenty-five years of loyal summer attendance. But the hotels cannot afford to grow old gracefully with their guests. Instead they must contrive to deny their ages with new programs that will appeal to and attract new generations of regular guests. Yet even the highly contemporary strategies developed to encourage new groups to discover the mountains — ecology retreats, cross-country skiing — echo long-standing resort traditions. Singles weekends label and structure the "opportunities" so tirelessly promoted by the anxious mothers and the social directors of earlier decades. Mohonk's "holistic way" only recasts its long-standing concern with promoting and providing recreation which engages the mind, body, and spirit of its guests. And somewhere in the foyers, gambling waits to introduce an element of risk into the history of the Catskill resorts, places which have for decades enclosed risk, and framed nature for the enjoyment of their guests.

—*Betsy Blackmar*

BETSY BLACKMAR, a social historian, is Assistant Professor of American Studies at Yale University. She is a member of the editorial collective of the *Radical History Review*.

John Margolies, 1978

On Vacation

The character of great resort areas like the Catskills has been tied intimately to the time and money available to their visitors. Resorts have been sustained by the patronage of those released, temporarily or otherwise, from the ordinary responsibilities of work, schooling, or homemaking. The visitors were all, in one way or another, on vacation.

Curiously, little has been written about the history of the American vacation and the methods evolved to ensure wage earners some leisure. The subject touches on so many of our values that a tentative survey might be useful.

Viewed across the last century and a half, the American vacation can be divided into four phases. They do not correspond easily to any obvious divisions of our history, but they reflect changing patterns of work, demography, and income distribution. Until the last third of the nineteenth century, the power to take time off for parts of the year, or to send one's family on trips for health or recreation, belonged almost exclusively to the wealthier classes. The great English and American spas which developed during the eighteenth and early nineteenth centuries were responding to the social needs of an agrarian and mercantile aristocracy. On a homelier level, the traditions of the great English watering places were repeated at White Sulphur Springs, Virginia; Saratoga, New York; and Bedford Springs, Pennsylvania. Seaside and mountain spots, like Cape May, New Jersey, and Brattleboro, Vermont, also began to lure weary, moneyed Americans for brief stays, decades before the Civil War.

George Templeton Strong, that cultivated New Yorker whose diary exposes so many details of upper-class life, grew up spending summers at Whitestone, in Flushing; in the 1840s, newly married, he began sending his wife to West Point, where she could not only enjoy the scenic Hudson views, but share the vigorous social life that flourished around the Military Academy. In the 1850s, his family summered, among other places, in Lenox, Nahant, and Great Barrington, Massachusetts, and in Brattleboro, Vermont. "Pity the metropolis should taint the country as it does for a circle of at least thirty miles radius around it," Strong reflected in 1851. The "civic scum" ebbed and flowed on weekends and holidays, infesting Long Island and Staten Island; "all conveniently accessible hotels and boarding houses are overrun by the vermin that hot weather roasts out of its homes in town." Coney Island was simply "Church Street transported bodily a few miles out of town."[1]

Strong's social standards and sense of status were probably more pronounced than those of most of his wealthy contemporaries, but his concern with company as well as climate reflected the air of privilege that surrounded the American vacationers of his time. While shopkeepers, workers, and apprentices could manage a day's excursion every now and again to the seashore, or take river trips and enjoy picnics, few Americans could afford long holidays or send their families to hotels or boarding houses for weeks at a time. Patriotic and religious holidays provided some relief from work, but it was unpaid relief, and the number of holidays in nineteenth-century America was much smaller than it had been in fifteenth- and sixteenth-century Europe.[2]

The idea of a regular, annual vacation, for all, remained unborn. Sending women and children off to escape the dangers of heat and disease was simply a prerogative of class, and so was joining them for a while during the dog days of August or September. Much business remained seasonal, so

CHILDREN'S PLAYING GROUND.

professionals and successful merchants could follow their clients and customers out of town, timing their idleness to match pauses in their work calendars. Recreation was not necessarily less valued than it is today, but the nation was still predominantly rural, and agricultural labor peaked during summer months. The value of hard and continuous work, moreover, was preached from both the pulpit and the counting house, and the development of a general philosophy of recreation seemed remote indeed.

Urban and industrial workers, of course, fought to control the demands of employment. During the Jacksonian era, the labor movement organized unsuccessfully to obtain an eight-hour day, while sabbatarians stressed the importance of keeping workers rested at least one day each week. The basic issues of wages and hours were so vital, however, and union weakness so obvious, that welfare matters received little attention from either employers or employees for most of the century. Besides, the spasmodic character of the economy, with the recurring booms and busts that punctuated nineteenth-century industrial life, made frequent unemployment the order of the day for many workers. While joblessness was never welcome, and often meant desperation, the economic slumps ironically served to interrupt the harsh discipline of daily labor, and a preindustrial work rhythm survived. The logic of the machine and the tyranny of the assembly line did not yet wholly dominate the work process.

The Privileged Vacation, for that was what leisure time in this era amounted to, began to weaken in the last third of the century and give way to a second phase which might be labeled the Commercialized Vacation. Its ingredients were present before the Civil War, but they grew in volume afterward, when a substantial portion of the labor market worked at clerical and bureaucratic tasks, serving burgeoning commercial and governmental enterprises. Although their work patterns were more genteel, they were soon subjected to the tight disciplines which governed the factory worker. Urban scale and congestion grew, not only in the East but in the Middle West as well. Railroad mileage increased more than sixfold between 1860 and 1900, accompanied by improved mass-transit systems that could carry urbanites quickly and inexpensively to the mass resort areas being built on city borders. Clearly there were profits to be made from organizing and packaging the leisure of this new middle class. And industrial profits were swelling the number of wealthy Americans who were now eager to join their predecessors in tasting the joys of leisure.

It was during this period that new institutions were created to regularize the business of travel and vacationing. Railroad companies appointed passenger agents to cope with the complexities of ticketing and to suggest the spectacular new vacation possibilities in the Far West; Thomas Cook & Sons began a flourishing American travel agency in the 1870s, followed in the next decades by Raymond & Whitcomb, "Ask Mr. Foster," the Colpitts Travel Company, and many others.[3] Guidebooks multiplied, more studiously evaluating the comforts of hotel establishments. Newspapers filled with vacation advertisements, and during the first decade of the twentieth century began their Sunday travel sections. In August, 1902, *The World's Week*, typifying the interest of mass magazines, devoted its entire August issue to play. "Simply as a business," it noted, "vacation has come to be one of the Great Industries," now "organized, classified, 'conducted,'" and "brought within the reach of every-

body."[4]

Along with the great hotels there now appeared private cottage colonies and bungalow groups. In the Adirondacks and the Thousand Islands, Anson Phelps Stokes, Alfred G. Vanderbilt, Timothy L. Woodruff, and others built luxurious cottages alongside remote mountain lakes.[5] Mackinac; Cedar Island in Lake Erie; Asheville, North Carolina; Harbor Springs and Petoskey in Michigan; Oconomoc, Wisconsin; and other spots distant from the familiar centers along the East Coast, ministered to the needs of vacationers. In only twenty years, wrote the librarian-reformer Melvil Dewey in 1895, a revolution in public sentiment had developed. The vacation was now recognized "not as a luxury, but as a necessity for those who aim to do a large amount of high-grade work."[6]

Moralists had always mistrusted the hothouse atmosphere of the great social resort, charging that its extravagance and indulgence infected not only the vacationers, but the simpler values of country life. "The flat for home and the hotel for vacation constitute the climax of social negativeness," E. P. Powell wrote in 1903, urging his readers to seek cottages and farmhouses instead of pretentious hotels for their diversion.[7] Resorts are "necessarily money-making in their inception," wrote the *Independent*, "an exploitation of all sorts of fads, and a certain social vulgarity which in the end must leave its stamp on every person who frequents them."[8] The great hotels were becoming merely "the summer homes of the class," the *Nation* had noted earlier, "while the remoter places are sought for by the mass."[9]

Whether in monster hotel or quiet farm retreat, the summer vacation seemed pervasive and inexorable to the middle-class journals of the day. During the 1870s, the word *vacation* became a verb as well as a noun; it was now an activity as well as a period of time. The vacation was benefiting from new attitudes toward leisure developing in America, a compound of several trends: a revulsion against a so-called Puritan antipathy toward pleasure; a growing cosmopolitanism concerning European traditions of holiday making and vacationing, fed by heavy immigration and expanding international travel; and, most of all, a new concern with efficiency in work, in family life, and in education, which defined the vacation as a conservative device to help strengthen basic social institutions. The pressures of modern life and machinery had made the vacation "a moral and physical necessity to the employee and a profitable indulgence by the employer," wrote one supporter of the movement.[10] If "a man has the right to work," the *Outlook* editorialized, "he has also a right to live. No man can work well unless he lives well," and no one lived well unless he received the things which nourished him.[11]

The growth of the middle-class vacation coincided, in the late nineteenth and early twentieth centuries, with the great wave of affection for wilderness and the natural landscape. Fishing and hunting clubs, the Boy Scouts, the popularity of animal stories, conservation societies, botanical gardens, zoos, municipal park systems, and garden clubs were among the many expressions of the urge, which was becoming a self-conscious response to the apparently inevitable and insatiable urbanizing process.[12] The custom of taking several weeks off each summer to return to a simpler, more fundamental relationship to nature appealed intensely when the vocabulary of nature was receiving so much rapturous expression from the nation's publicists.

But there existed two serious tensions, despite

the idyllic descriptions. One concerned the meaning of the vacation itself. The other involved the vacationers.

Many critics noted the contradiction between a desire for rest and a conscience-stricken insistence upon extracting benefits from any activity, work or play. "We inherited from our strenuous ancestors a belief that loafing is a sin, so for most of us yet an excuse for idleness is necessary," the *Independent* explained.[13] The typical American, Baron de Stampenbourg commented in the same journal, was "so doggedly bent on making every day tell in fun for every month spent at work that the fun-procuring becomes an enterprise," forbidding rest.[14] An added problem was the increasing specialization of modern life which, according to some, had "destroyed the ability to find relaxation in a change of occupation." Most participated in "but a narrow round of activity, and, this coming to an end, we are stranded, bored, and disappointed."[15] Trivial amusements seemed the almost universal drug.

But even if nature was restorative, and the simplicities of mountain air, deserted forest, and solitary walks could encourage a more healthy set of values, new problems arose. For when Americans flocked to see nature's charms for themselves, they inevitably created traffic jams. Gregarious in their play as in their work, they turned the secret places of the land into little cities, after burdening them with romantic names. "The desire for solitary communion with nature is so great that people flock in crowds to any place where it may be enjoyed," the *Independent* complained in 1903. "To discover some spot where nature is yet unadorned and then to adorn it is the occupation of the resorter."[16] Hugh Pendexter estimated in 1913 that the United States contained at least two hundred thousand Lovers' Leaps, in addition to thousands of Devil's Washbowls.[17]

The other major problem with the Commercialized Vacation concerned its consumers. For, despite the boasting of national participation, the ability to take several weeks off and spend them in the countryside was severely limited in the era before World War I.[18] While the aristocrats of skilled labor—unionized construction workers, for example—might earn enough to support a week's vacation, few others reached this height. Salaried industrial workers were largely excluded from the experience. Immigrant workers saved desperately to send their wives and children to the country, but this was hardly the kind of leisurely touring and family togetherness that the middle-class journals were promoting. That awaited a minor revolution which would help usher in a third phase of the American institution: the annual paid vacation.

By World War I, millions of clerks and bureaucrats were enjoying salaried one- or two-week vacations, and in 1916 federal workers received the right to annual vacations of up to thirty days. But it was not until the 1920s that any significant extension of this system was made to factory workers, and even then it was slow and spasmodic. However, the development of the trend, and increasing reliance upon the automobile as a method of reaching American vacationlands spelled a new era. The Commercialized Vacation, with its packaged touring, its vast hotels, amusement parks, and bungalow colonies, now gave way to the Industrial Vacation, a worldwide movement prompted, in part, by the increasing militance of the labor movement, flowering first in Europe and finally blossoming in America in the 1940s and 1950s.

Before World War I, some industrial firms, headed by benevolent or audacious capitalists, had

CARGILL & ALDRICH'S
LIVERY STABLES,
In New Brick Building,
Two doors North of Irving House,
Maine Street,
CATSKILL, N. Y.
This is the most extensive Livery in Town, and can furnish Rigs in all Styles.

experimented with the notion of vacations for factory workers. The owners accepted the universal need for annual rest, and also believed that they could reduce turnover and increase labor stability by the device.[19] In Britain, legislation was introduced to clarify the situation; the Factory Act of 1901 established six statutory holidays each year, for women and young people under eighteen. The holidays were often extended to men, but they were holidays without pay. A few national unions in Britain, notably the railway workers and printers, bargained to obtain short, annual paid vacations as part of their contracts. But they were not typical.

The active and aggressive notion of paid vacations as a worker's right did not develop until after the war, when many Continental governments with active socialist participation stipulated by law that each worker was entitled to a certain number of paid vacation days each year. According to Charles Mills's 1927 survey, only France and Belgium, among major industrial countries, lagged behind in the European vacation movement.[20] While the British government did not establish the same kinds of requirements set up in Austria, Czechoslovakia, Denmark, and Italy, dozens of national unions negotiated contracts guaranteeing paid vacations. By 1925, more than one and a half million British workers were covered by such contracts. In Germany, 92 percent of the workers covered by collective agreements received annual vacations; in Sweden, 77 percent, in the Netherlands, 54 percent — all this by the middle of the 1920s.

In the United States, however, progress was much slower. The *Monthly Labor Review*, published by the Bureau of Labor Statistics, periodically monitored the vacation benefits of industrial workers. Its first study, made in 1916, found that only 16 of the 389 establishments it queried granted paid vacations to shop or salaried workers. Ten years later the situation had changed, but only partially. Of some 250 firms — including manufacturers, department stores, banks, and insurance companies — almost 40 percent now granted paid vacations to hourly workers, although almost all plans were tied to continuous service by the employee, most of them demanding at least one year of work to qualify for the largess.[21]

As awareness of the enormous gaps between the benefits of government and private-sector employees developed during the decade, industrial workers increased their demands for the same rights that civil-service and clerical staffs already possessed and that European workers now treated as a matter of course. In 1928, the *Nation* published an explosive editorial charging that the American vacation was founded on fraud and hypocrisy, "a grotesque collection of habits based upon class power and perpetuated by inertia." Noting that a recent New York State Department of Labor investigation of 1,500 factories revealed that 91 percent of them gave paid vacations to office workers and only 18 percent to production workers, the *Nation* declared the philosophy behind this to be absurd. Apparently "men and women who work with their brains are sensitive, fine-strung, in constant need of replenishing burned-out energy," while those who "work primarily with their hands are stolid, ox-like, in need of a thick beefsteak and a sound sleep to prepare them adequately for the next day's work." This theory of labor held no more truth "than the superstitions once held by historians concerning the fine blood and biological gentility of the aristocracy." All who worked needed vacations, the *Nation* argued, and none more than those who worked with their hands. Fatigue would

VIEW FROM SUNSET ROCK.

destroy the mind and body of a ditchdigger "just as surely as it will destroy the mind and body of a bank president."[22]

But despite these arguments and the European precedents, most American unions continued to concentrate their demands on raising hourly wages. The coming of the Depression and widespread unemployment undoubtedly delayed any further advances in vacation legislation, so it was not really until World War II, with its massive influx of female factory workers, its wage controls, and its chronic labor scarcities, that the vacation became truly general. While the statistical record is complicated, there is some indication that fewer than 10 percent of those covered by union agreements were getting a two-week paid vacation by 1940, but by 1944 this had risen to a majority, and by 1949, to 90 percent.[23] In a perspective that survives into the present, management still regarded the paid vacation as a privilege, to be doled out in terms of loyal service. In many firms, as much as five years of steady employment were necessary to qualify for these two weeks. The principle would become more generously interpreted in the years ahead, as health and vacation benefits figured more prominently in collective bargaining.

The addition of millions of industrial workers to the ranks of annual vacationers, then, was not as rapid as might have seemed likely at the beginning of the 1920s. But the easy notion that almost every employed American worker could afford to take an annual vacation was at last matched by reality as the 1940s ended. As automobile ownership became so widespread that it produced its own subculture, the Industrial Vacation, like most consumer products, was mass-produced and marketed aggressively. And the resulting strain of numbers on facilities emphasized the need for better planning, and rewarded initiative in seeking the unbeaten path.

The widespread participation that characterized the Industrial Vacation was not, however, the permanent phase. It was succeeded by still another form which simultaneously encompassed and transcended the previous three. The symbol of the Privileged Vacation might well be the private country house or the grand hotel to which the leisured classes could retire for months at a time. The Commercialized Vacation featured the travel agent and the railroad train, and their collaborative product, the packaged outing; and the emblem of the Industrial Vacation was the automobile, with its motel culture and perpetual touring. But the country house, the packaged vacation, and the automobile were to be brought together in the twin symbols of this fourth and contemporary phase — the airplane, with its promise to conquer distance, and the weekend house, the second home, and its lure of instant year-round retreat from the cares and pressures of urban life. Just as the organized package tour depended on the airplane, the weekend home required the use of an automobile and reflected a sense, popular in the 1960s, that shorter work weeks, made possible by increasing productivity, could make the vacation a year-round activity. And, in fact, the increasing popularity of winter sports like skiing, and more exotic warm-weather diversions like skin diving, as well as the continuing enthusiasm for golf and tennis, led to many second homes planned around the accessibility to sports.

This current phase might be termed the Boundless Vacation, for it refused to obey the temporal and seasonal limits which had previously hedged the annual respites. Not only was the entire world thrust open for exploration, but now it was the

entire year that offered possibilities for escape. Improved travel has made it possible to accomplish vacation feats in a fortnight that once required six months or more. The sale of vans and campers, the crowds at museums and historical sites, the growth of gambling resorts, the Disneyland phenomenon, the complex pattern of charter flights, investment in vacation condominiums for rental during peak seasons, changing modes of conventioneering, these testify to the new varieties in American vacations. Brief, informal trips to summer homes and weekend houses meant that individuals or families could choose several kinds of holidays each year, varying short rests from work with longer, more ambitious trips to distant places.

But the confident expectations of more leisure, which in the fifties and sixties stimulated a flurry of special studies and reports on the "leisure problem," were not always fulfilled.[24] Sociologists analyzing the changing work week found that commuting was cutting deeply into the extra hours obtained by many American workers. The spreading net of suburbanization and crowded highways made the daily chore increasingly onerous, particularly when it was combined with deteriorating mass-transit systems. Airports tended to become congested and disagreeable during holidays and peak hours; long-distance planning was necessary to avoid disappointment and extra cost.

The rise of the four-day week was inexplicably delayed, and the apparently permanent energy crisis raised the price of movement. Depreciating or unstable dollar values made international travel a forbidding, and sometimes even humiliating experience for the budget-minded. The vacation process now required levels of synchronization and decision-making as complex as those required at work. Nevertheless, the Boundless Vacation did represent some fundamental shifts, for the flexibility of the calendar, and the easier transition between work and play, broadened and diversified our notions of time off.

However popular the vacation and its resorts have become, they have never assumed the importance in this country that they hold in Europe. Our commitment to the work ethic remains more powerful, and a freer spending tradition has given Americans more diversified ways to indicate status and economic achievement than simply vacation consumership. The early success of European unions in gaining paid vacations, and the dramatic exodus of European urban workers to country retreats each summer, are as much functions of this difference in values as they are of a politically active labor movement.

But the American resort was never, like its European counterpart, a temporal alternative to settled community; it is rather a spatial and emotional surrogate, a substitute for a world where rules and assumptions no longer make sense of experience. Artificial and exaggerated as many may have been, American resorts, either skewed toward the simple life or tilted toward sybaritism, have presented to many patrons a vision of security and coherence, an anniversary institution to measure the passing of time, extending a familial vision more intense than strained family ties could support. For them, being on vacation was fulfilling a destiny otherwise inaccessible, and the resort hotel was their world to conquer. In a sense then, from the day of the Privileged Vacation through the apparently limitless horizons of the Boundless Vacation, the Catskills have always been involved with American dreams; only the images have changed.

—Neil Harris

Notes

[1]Allan Nevins and Milton Halsey Thomas, eds., *The Diary of George Templeton Strong* (New York: 1952), vol. II, p. 61.

[2]*The Monthly Labor Review* XXII (June, 1926), pp. 41–45, talks of the shrinkage in holiday time from late medieval to modern times. See also Robert W. Malcolmson, *Popular Recreations In English Society, 1700–1850* (Cambridge, England: 1973), chapters 1–2.

[3]Many of these trends are described in Hugh De Santis, "The Democratization of Travel: The Travel Agent in American History," *Journal of American Culture* I (Spring, 1978), pp. 1–19.

[4]"The People At Play," *The World's Week* IV (August, 1902), pp. 2373–77. Other essays in that issue were entitled "The City as a Summer Resort" and "One State and the 'Summer People Industry,'" a report of the New Hampshire Commissioner of Labor. See also Lawrence Perry, "The Business of Vacations," *World's Week* VI (June, 1903), pp. 3506–16; Edward Hungerford, "Our Summer Migration. A Social Study," *Century* XLII (August, 1891), pp. 569–76; and "Summer Resorters," *Independent* LV (August 27, 1903), pp. 2069–70.

[5]William Frederick Dix, "Summer Life in Luxurious Adirondack Camps," *Independent* LV (July 2, 1903), 1556–62.

[6]Melvil Dewey, "Co-operation in Vacations," *Outlook* LII (July 27, 1895), p. 135. For the multiplication of resorts across the country, see two articles by Harrison Rhodes, "American Holidays. The Sea-Shore," *Harper's Magazine* CXXIX (June, 1914), pp. 3–15; and "American Holidays. Fresh Water and Inland Valleys," *Harper's Magazine* CXXIX (July, 1914), pp. 211–21.

[7]E. P. Powell, "A Simple Vacation," *Independent* LV (June 4, 1903), p. 1324.

[8]"Private vs. Public Resorts," *Independent* LIII (June 6, 1901), p. 1332.

[9]"Changes in Summer Migration," *The Nation* LIII (September 17, 1891), p. 210. For other assaults on the great resorts see Julian Ralph, "The Moral Soundness of American Life," *The World's Work* V (November, 1902), pp. 2747–49; and "Summer Pleasures for the American," *New York Times*, August 26, 1876, p. 4.

[10]Baron de Stampenbourg, "Spending a Vacation, Here and Abroad," *Independent* LV (June 4, 1903), p. 1301.

[11]"Vacations for Everybody," *Outlook* LXXI (May 31, 1902), p. 304. See also "The Need for Vacations," *Independent* LXXII (June 20, 1912), pp. 1388–89.

[12]The best summary of this movement can be found in Peter J. Schmitt, *Back to Nature* (New York: 1969).

[13]"Summer Resorters," *Independent* LV (August 27, 1903), p. 2069.

[14]Baron de Stampenbourg, "Spending a Vacation, Here and Abroad," *Independent* LV (June 4, 1903), p. 1301.

[15]*Outlook* CII (October 5, 1912), p. 273.

[16]"Summer Resorters," *Independent* LV (August 27, 1903), p. 2070.

[17]Hugh Pendexter, "I Hear You Calling Me," *Everybody's Magazine* XXVIII (June, 1913), pp. 752–57.

[18]For an example of the boasting see Franklin Matthews, "Vacations for the Workers," *The World's Work* VI (June, 1903), pp. 3516–20.

[19]The vacation was part of a system of "welfare capitalism" developing in the late nineteenth century, although a recent study, Stuart D. Brandes, *American Welfare Capitalism, 1880–1940* (Chicago: 1976), does not discuss the vacation at all.

[20]Charles M. Mills, *Vacations For Industrial Workers*, Part III (New York: 1927). Mills's book was summarized in the *Monthly Labor Review* XXV (September, 1927), p. 49.

[21]"Vacations With Pay For Wage Earners," *Monthly Labor Review* XXII (May, 1926), pp. 1–7. See also a study of vacation policies in Cincinnati, "Vacations with Pay for Production Workers," *Monthly Labor Review* XXIII (July, 1926), pp. 35–36; and Grace Pugh, "Vacations with Pay," *Survey* L (July 15, 1923), pp. 435–36.

[22]"Vacations," *The Nation* CXXVII (September 5, 1928), p. 215.

[23]Benjamin L. Masse, "Vacations with Pay," *America* XCV (June 30, 1956), p. 315. The National Industrial Conference Board surveys suggested a somewhat higher proportion of companies granting vacations to all employees before World War II, but the summary in *Business Week* (June 22, 1957), p. 111, did not indicate the proportion of the work force actually receiving vacations. The American Federation of Labor *Historical Encyclopedia and Reference Book*, III, part 2, (Washington, D.C.: 1960), p. 2478, placed the beginning of the movement for vacations with pay for wage-earners in 1937. In 1947 the A.F. of L. endorsed a goal of twenty-six days of annual paid vacation for union contracts.

[24]Magazines in the late fifties and early sixties were filled with articles discussing the "leisure problem" which, in retrospect, seem amusingly naive. A useful assemblage of articles, some of them rather critical of the notion that leisure was becoming so widespread as to be dangerous, can be found in Eric Larrabee and Rolf Meyersohn, eds., *Mass Leisure* (Glencoe, Illinois: 1958).

NEIL HARRIS, Professor of History at the University of Chicago, has written extensively on American popular taste, from housing to art and entertainment. He is the author of *Humbug: The Art of P.T. Barnum*.

References

BOOKS

The most complete overview of the history of the Catskills region is Alf Evers, *The Catskills: From Wilderness to Woodstock*, New York: 1972. For the history of Sullivan County resorts, see Manville B. Wakefield, *To the Mountains by Rail*, Grahamsville, New York: 1970. For the history of Greene County's first great resort hotel, see Roland Van Zandt, *The Catskill Mountain House: The Birth, Glory, and Death of the Great Hudson Valley Hotel Which Symbolized the American Romantic Era*, New Brunswick, New Jersey: 1966. Contemporary accounts of nineteenth-century Catskills resorts can be found in numerous travel guides such as Theodore Dwight, *Northern Traveler, Containing the Routes to Niagara, Quebec, and the Springs*, New York: 1825; Robert Vandewater, *The Tourist: A Pocket Manual for Travelers*, New York: 1934; and in the delightful and sardonic George W. Curtis, *Lotus Eating: A Summer Book*, New York: 1852.

For descriptions of settlement and social life in the Catskills in the late nineteenth and early twentieth century see A. E. P. Searing's *Land of Rip Van Winkle*, New York: 1884; Gabriel Davidson, *Our Jewish Farmers and the Story of the Jewish Agricultural Society*, New York: 1943. On twentieth-century resorts see Joey Adams, with Henry Tobias, *The Borscht Belt*, New York: 1966; and Joel Pomeranz, *Jennie and the Story of Grossinger's*, New York: 1970.

Recent histories of river and rail travel contain helpful details about resort life: Gerald Best, *The Ulster and Delaware: Railroad through the Catskills*, San Marino, California: 1972; William Helmer, *O & W, The Long Life and Slow Death of the New York, Ontario & Western Railway*, Berkeley, California: 1959; and Donald Ringwald, *The Hudson River Day Line*, New York: 1965.

Recent studies concerned with the ecology of the Catskill region help to place resort life in context: *The Future of the Catskills*, Final Report of the Temporary State Commission to Study the Catskills, Albany: 1975; and Peter Borelli, ed., *The Catskill Center Plan*, Hobart; 1974, both available through the Catskill Center, Hobart, New York.

County guides are a general source of information. They usually include details about every important person or place in the county or locale, including hotels. Examples are John H. French, *Gazetteer of the State of New York*, 8th ed., Syracuse: 1860; Francis P. Kimball, *The Capital Region of the State of New York*, New York: 1942; James Quinlan, *History of Sullivan County*, Liberty, New York: 1873, repr. 1966; F. W. Beers, *Atlas of Ulster County*, New York: 1875, repr. 1975; F. W. Beers, *History of Greene County*, New York: 1884, repr. 1969; W. W. Munsell, *History of Delaware County*, Albany: 1880, repr. 1976; and Katherine Terwilliger, *Wawarsing — Where the Streams Wind*, Ellenville, New York: 1977.

BROCHURES and TOUR GUIDES

Much of the information in these essays comes from the numerous travel guides and promotional brochures issued by individual hotels and railroad companies. Thorough listings of the hotels as well as richly descriptive advertisements can be found in the *Summer Homes* series issued annually by the New York, Ontario & Western Railway from 1878 through the early 1930s; in Walton Van Loan, *Catskill Mountain Guide*, 1879–1915; and in the Ulster and Delaware Railroad annual guides to resorts in Greene and Delaware Counties: *The Catskill Mountains*, 1891–1920s. Also useful are: Harper's *New York and Erie Railroad Guidebook* for the 1850s and earlier; William Williams, *The Canal and Steamboat Register . . . for 1830; The New York State Tourist*, New York: 1842; Kirk Munroe, *Summer in the Catskill Mountains*, New York, Buffalo, and West Shore Railroad Company, 1883; Lippincott's *Illustrated Guide Book to the Principal Summer Resorts of the United States*, New York: 1876; and E. B. Van Aken, *Guide to Catskills and Vicinity*, 1881. The *Picturesque Catskills* series, published by R. Lionel deLisser in the 1890s, focuses on scenic attractions.

Collections of individual hotel brochures and regional guides can be found at the New York Historical Society; the Local History and Genealogy Collection of the New

York Public Library; Avery Library, Columbia University; the Greene County Historical Society; Haines Falls Free Library; the Mohonk Barn Museum; and in the private collections of Alf Evers, Shady, New York; and Barbara Purcell, the Manville Wakefield Collection, Grahamsville, New York.

ARTICLES and NEWSPAPERS

Articles of particular use in writing these essays were Alice Hyneman Rhine, "Race Prejudice at Summer Resorts," *The Forum*, July, 1887; James Ford, "The Old Fashioned Summer Hotel," *Munsey's Magazine*, March 21, 1899; "Mohonk and Its Conferences," *New England Magazine*, June, 1897; "My Mother Said I Should Give It a Try," *Saturday Evening Post*, October 8, 1966; Mordecai Richler, "The Catskills: Land of Milk and Money," *Holiday*, July, 1965.

Notes on the summer season at Catskill hotels appeared regularly in the *New York Times* and the *New York Herald* from the late 1870s through the 1920s. The vacation supplement of the *Brooklyn Daily Eagle*, vol. 22, no. 2, February, 1905, contains nice descriptions of the attractions of Catskill boarding houses. Also of particular interest are *New York Times* articles on "Vacations for Working Girls," July 16, 1909; "How Long Should a Man's Vacation Be?" July 31, 1910; and on comparisons between European and American working-class vacations, August 30, 1931. The Haines Falls Free Library, the Greene County Historical Society, Barbara Purcell's Manville Wakefield collection, and Alf Evers's private collection all contain extensive clippings files from local Catskill newspapers reporting resort activity. Of particular interest are clippings from the Liberty *Register*, the *Liberty Herald*, the Greene County *News*, and the *Catskill Examiner*.

MANUSCRIPTS

One of the most vivid personal accounts of life in the Catskills appears in the *Diary of Charles Baldwin* (1866–1884) in the Manuscripts Collection of the New York State Library at Albany. Other diaries describe visits to the Catskills as part of the Grand Tour or as an annual summer experience. These include diaries by Marguerite DuBois (1907–1908), Joanna Anthon (1867–1883), Amy L. Waters (1907–1911), and Robert Taylor (1844), all available in the Manuscripts Collection of the New York Public Library.

BIBLIOGRAPHY for ARCHITECTURE

Literature on Catskill architecture is hard to come by, and building plans are almost unobtainable. For general background on hotels see Leslie Dorsey and Janice Devine, *Fare Thee Well: A Backward Look at Two Centuries of Historic American Hostelries*, New York: 1964; Elsie Lathrop, *Early American Inns and Taverns*, New York: 1937; Arthur S. White, *Palaces of the People: A Social History of Commercial Hospitality*, New York: 1970; and Jeffrey Limerick, "The Grand Resort Hotels of America," *Perspecta 15*, 1975. On the verandah, see Clay Lancaster, "The American Bungalow," *Art Bulletin*, September, 1958; and Niklaus Pevsner, *A History of Building Types*, Princeton: 1976. For the specific hotels, illustration is available in railroad guides, tourist albums, and the pamphlets and advertisements issued by the hotels themselves. Also see Elizabeth Cromley, "Upward and Inward with Time: Resorts of the Catskills," *Progressive Architecture*, February, 1978.

LITERARY SOURCES

Life in the Catskills over the last two hundred years has left its imprint on American literature, ranging from the works of Washington Irving and James Fenimore Cooper to Philip Roth and Isaac Bashevis Singer. Irving's tales, "Rip Van Winkle" and "The Legend of Sleepy Hollow," *The Legend of Sleepy Hollow and Other Tales*, Tarrytown, New York: 1974; and Cooper's *The Pioneers*, New York: 1825, gave an early aura of legend to the Catskills and were often circulated by Catskill publicists. Comments by Cooper, Irving, William Cullen Bryant, and others were published in David Murdoch's anthology *The Scenery of the Catskill Mountains*, New York: 1846. Roland Van Zandt has also edited a collection of literary comments on the region in *Chronicles of the Hudson: Three Centuries of Travelers' Accounts*, New Brunswick, New Jersey: 1971. Other books that capture the spirit of the resorts are Abraham Cahan, *The Rise of David Levinsky*, New York: 1917; Herman Wouk, *Marjorie Morningstar*, Garden City, New York: 1955; and Moss Hart, *Act One*, New York: 1959. Arthur Kober set his 1937 play, *Having Wonderful Time*, at a camp in the mountains; and Gertrude Berg's NBC radio series of the 1930s, "House of Glass," recreated life in a small, family-run Catskill hotel.

Index

(Page numbers in *italics* indicate photographs)